PUFFIN BOOKS
WILD IN THE BACKYARD

Arefa Tehsin spent her childhood treading the Aravali jungles with her naturalist father. As a child, she was often found trying to catch a snake or spin a yarn. She grew up to be a storyteller and was appointed the Honorary Wildlife Warden of Udaipur for a term. She is the author of several fiction and non-fiction books for children and young adults, and writes columns and articles for various national dailies and magazines. A dreamer and rationalist, she is a serial traveller who wants to go on an endless journey starting with planet earth. (Irrational for a rationalist? Ask her companion, Aditya!)

WILD IN THE BACKYARD

AREFA TEHSIN

PUFFIN BOOKS

PUFFIN BOOKS
Published by the Penguin Group
Penguin Books India Pvt. Ltd, 7th Floor, Infinity Tower C, DLF Cyber City,
Gurgaon 122 002, Haryana, India
Penguin Group (USA) Inc., 375 Hudson Street, New York, New York 10014, USA
Penguin Group (Canada), 90 Eglinton Avenue East, Suite 700, Toronto,
Ontario, M4P 2Y3, Canada
Penguin Books Ltd, 80 Strand, London WC2R 0RL, England
Penguin Ireland, 25 St Stephen's Green, Dublin 2, Ireland (a division of
Penguin Books Ltd)
Penguin Group (Australia), 707 Collins Street, Melbourne, Victoria 3008, Australia
Penguin Group (NZ), 67 Apollo Drive, Rosedale, Auckland 0632, New Zealand
Penguin Books (South Africa) (Pty) Ltd, Block D, Rosebank Office Park,
181 Jan Smuts Avenue, Parktown North, Johannesburg 2193, South Africa

Penguin Books Ltd, Registered Offices: 80 Strand, London WC2R 0RL, England

First published in Puffin by Penguin Books India 2015

Text copyright © Arefa Tehsin 2015
Illustration copyright © Sayantan Halder

All rights reserved

10 9 8 7 6 5 4 3 2 1

The views and opinions expressed in this book are the author's own and the facts are as reported by him which have been verified to the extent possible, and the publishers are not in any way liable for the same.

ISBN 9780143333906

Typeset in Avenir by Manipal Digital Systems, Manipal
Printed at Thomson Press India Ltd, New Delhi

This book is sold subject to the condition that it shall not, by way of trade or otherwise, be lent, resold, hired out, or otherwise circulated without the publisher's prior written consent in any form of binding or cover other than that in which it is published and without a similar condition including this condition being imposed on the subsequent purchaser and without limiting the rights under copyright reserved above, no part of this publication may be reproduced, stored in or introduced into a retrieval system, or transmitted in any form or by any means (electronic, mechanical, photocopying, recording or otherwise), without the prior written permission of both the copyright owner and the above-mentioned publisher of this book.

A PENGUIN RANDOM HOUSE COMPANY

To my father, who took me to the bookstore and the jungle, who held my hand, yet left me alone. At both places.

In the end we will conserve only what we love, we will love only what we understand, and we will understand only what we are taught.

– Baba Dioum

CONTENTS

Introduction ix

Chapter 1	The Devil's Own	1
Chapter 2	The Dreamcatchers	13
Chapter 3	The Serpent Hunters	25
Chapter 4	Blissfully Blind	33
Chapter 5	Oh, Them Bloodsuckers	39
Chapter 6	More Bloodsuckers	45
Chapter 7	Crafty Crows	51
Chapter 8	The Super Survivors	57
Chapter 9	Fluttering Fairies	65
Chapter 10	The Black Lord of the Skies	75
Chapter 11	Monkey Lore	81
Chapter 12	Lousy Lice	91
Chapter 13	The Hundred Legger	99
Chapter 14	The Thousand Legger	107
Chapter 15	The Hyper Little Birdies	115
Chapter 16	The Matey Masses	123
Chapter 17	The Silent Killer	133
Chapter 18	Wall-G	141
Chapter 19	The Shadow-Tailed	149
Chapter 20	The Untamed Shrew	159

CONTENTS

Chapter 21	The Hopper Gangs	165
Chapter 22	Rats! Who is that?	173
Chapter 23	Backyard Beauties	187
Chapter 24	The Slimy and the Sluggish	209
Chapter 25	The Backyard Probe	217

Acknowledgements 229
Books To Read 230

INTRODUCTION

We may think that wilderness and wildlife are confined to forests. But there is a whole lot of wild in our own backyards. Do you know, when animals and plants share the same living space, it is called an ecosystem? Discover the animals that share your city's ecosystem and your home—there are the hunters and the hunted, the diggers and the tunnellers, raptors and roaches, the eight-legged and the legless, with their canines and claws, growls and chirps . . . There's a lost world all around us.

There are many creatures that have got used to our noisy and clumsy habits. There are garden and house lizards, harmless shrews and blind snakes, watchful kites and yogic grasshoppers, savvy roaches and hurrying rats, hard-working earthworms and sly skinks, pi-oooo-singing koels and whoooo-hooting owls, gossipy sparrows and gloomy crows, blistering blister beetles and killer houseflies, swanky spiders and busybody ants, soulful toads and finless silverfish, skilful tailorbirds and loud-mouthed babblers, trendy butterflies and blood-sucking mosquitoes, lice in your head and bugs in your bed, slimy slugs and laid-back snails, scary millipedes and no-nonsense hornets, ghostly bats and un-dragon dragonflies . . . We have these and many other furry, scaly, feathery residents and neighbours. They could be burrowing under the soft garden grass or roosting on the bougainvillea bushes, hunting on the mango trees or fighting on the gulmohars, hiding in your kitchens or dating on your walls, dancing around your lights or jeering on your porch, silent in one season, chattering in another . . . Let's say hi to them and take a look at their home, which, by the way, is also ours.

THE DEVIL'S OWN

Of all the creatures that live in our backyards, walls, porches, gardens, hedges, trees, drains, beds and heads, these are the greatest hangers—they do a great job of hanging around. And no, we're not talking about your class monitor whom you call Locket because she always hangs around your neck!

This is a creature of the night. In many cultures it is linked with death, the devil and the dark underworld. Its hands are its wings—rubbery, flappy and webbed. It doesn't sleep on the ground like a mammal or sit on a branch like a bird. It hangs upside down—hiding its body with its dark, leathery wings—and looks at the upturned world with its mousy face. We've made it both a superhero and a supervillain: Batman and Dracula. The only mammal in the world that can fly—yep, you guessed it—the bat!

MICRO AND MEGA

These mammals have been able to spread across almost the entire world because they could fly. (Let's not imagine where else we humans would spread to if *we* had wings!) After rodents, bats make the biggest chunk of mammals in the world (about 20 per cent).

There are more than 1200 kinds of bats in the world and are divided mainly into two categories:

- microbats
- megabats

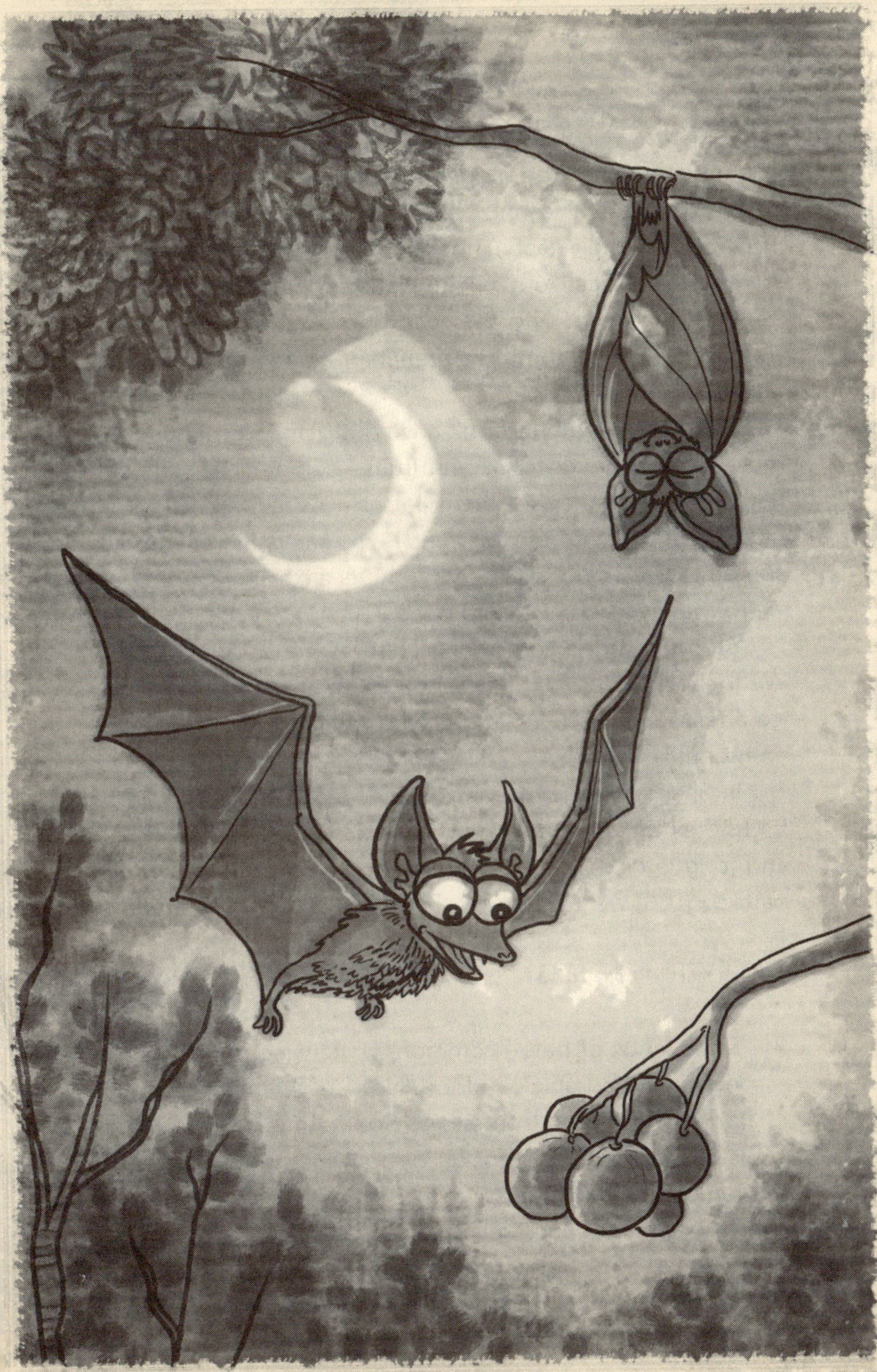

WILD IN THE BACKYARD

The megabats may be bigger in size but the micros are the ones with style. The microbats use echolocation to hunt. They locate their tasty meal through their high-pitched squeaks—they call out in the dark and their super-sharp ears get the echo. And they can make out from the echo, even in the dark, if there is a branch or a bird or a tiny insect ahead.

Since the megabats don't have this glam way of hunting, most of them prefer to just eat fruits—some micro ones eat fruits too—and a few of them eat fish. As for that question niggling at the back of your mind—you know, the one about something red and sticky—yes, there are vampire bats as well, who feed on . . . well, blood!

Blood or no blood, many cultures consider bats evil. We'll check out a few batty beliefs as we read along. So go ahead and read. What are you waiting for—the bats to come out?

In Shakespeare's *Macbeth*, the Three Witches add bat's fur to their brew—'Eye of newt and toe of frog / Wool of bat and tongue of dog . . .' They add some other gross animal parts too, but we'll leave it at that.

A BAGGY BAGFUL OF BAT FACTS

1. Three kinds of bats—common, white-winged and hairy-legged—feed only on blood. None of them are found in India. They live in Central and South America. And there is no badge of merit for guessing what they are called—vampire bats, of course.

2. Megabats are also called flying foxes. The wings of the giant golden-crowned flying fox can reach up to 5 ft 7 in., while the smallest of them all is the Kitti's hog-nosed bat—as tiny as 29–34 mm!
3. Since bats have to work hard to get their food and can't just pick it up from the supermarket, they eat a lot of things that you and I may not like to eat (or drink). For instance—

- Raw fish. They locate the ripples in the water with echolocation and—splash! There's your dish of fish.
- Frogs, lizards and birds. The top carnivores (meat-eaters) of the bat world eat them. The American false vampire bat and the Australian ghost bat feed on other bats. If you were top bully of the class, maybe you'd eat other students' lunches too . . . hmmm . . . hopefully not other students, though!
- Fruits. Well, you eat them too, don't you? But not in the same way bats do. They scatter the seeds—spitting pips along the way as they fly, munching—from which baby fruit trees grow. More than 150 kinds of trees depend on bats to grow. And what do we do? We just throw the seeds in our dustbins.
- Juicy insects. Some bats that can't echolocate catch insects by the sounds they make.
  Insect: Trrrr . . . trrrr . . . I was calling my wife, not you, you saw-toothed monst-er . . . er . . . er . . .
  Other kinds of bats catch and eat insects mid-air. They use their 'bug nets'—their tail and wings—to catch them.

Then they return to their roosting place with their meal. They use their tail membrane as a napkin so that bits of their meal don't fall on the ground. Now, can you beat these table manners?

- Blood. The vampires have drunk enough of it to earn their deadly name.
- Nectar and pollen of flowers. It is the favourite food of some bats. These bats help with pollinating flowers. The tube-lipped nectar bat has such a long tongue to drink nectar with that it keeps its tongue curled up inside its ribcage! It has a longer tongue than any other mammal of its size. I haven't heard of anyone else's tongue curling up in their ribcage, for heaven's sake!

4. Sometimes, bats make tents for themselves by biting leaves! They prefer to roost in old, haunted-looking buildings, hollows of trees, dark caves, or the thick banyan or peepul tree in your backyard or street. There may be times when you find a bat dangling dead from an electricity wire. The poor fellows confuse them for harmless branches at times and end up being roasted.
5. The meaning of 'bat' is associated with 'mouse' in many languages. Let's look at these examples, shall we?

- French: *Chauve-souris*   bald mouse
- Bosnian: *slijepimiš*   blind mouse
- Afrikaans: *vlermuis*   winged mouse
- Estonian: *nahkhiir*   leather mouse

- Spanish: *murciélago* blind mouse
- Old English: Flittermouse

See what I mean?

6. Bats either live alone or with roost-mates. Some bat caves can have millions of bats! They sleep and pick their lice in the dark of their caves. And talk to each other as well.
   Bat 1: Hey, I caught a bullfrog tonight! Yummy and fleshy! What about you?
   Bat 2: Oh, I just had ol' Fleabag—our bat neighbour from the tree below. And he was full of fleas!
7. Some bats found in cold regions travel hundreds of kilometres to warmer places in the winter. Others just spend their winters sleeping in their cosy caves. The hip word for their long winter sleep is hibernation. Don't you wish you could hibernate just before your exams? (*'Mommy, don't bother waking me up early tomorrow for school. I will be hibernating.'*) See, that's the advantage of learning hip words!
   They prefer not to fly in the rain. Their echoes from all the raindrops would drive them mad!
8. Bats may eat insects or lizards or even other bats. But they get eaten in turn too. There are bat hawks and bat falcons who love a good bat meal. And wait, it's not just these big birds of prey that hunt bats—even some big spiders like their bat snack. If a small bat got caught in a big spiderweb, it would soon find its way to bat heaven through the spider's stomach.

9. Bat poop is called guano. Just thought you'd like to know. Farmers at places collect it and use it as a fertilizer in their fields. Guano was used to make gunpowder during the US Civil War. To know how much power guano has, we'd have to see a bat fart.
10. Bats can live for more than twenty years. But they have only one pup at a time. They may be found in millions but their numbers are slowly going down. They are losing their homes. Besides, some people eat them too.
11. Nearly two-thirds of the world's bats eat insects. They are natural pest controllers. A thousand bats can eat four tons of insects every year! They eat one-third of their body weight in insects every night! If we didn't have bats, we'd have insects coming out of our mouths and noses (and not just out of our bathroom drains).

> *Did you know...*
>
> The Congress Avenue Bridge in Texas is the summer home of 15,00,000 Mexican free-tailed bats! Around 1,00,000 people come to this bridge every year at dusk to see these bats wake and yawn and leave their roost. It is the largest bat colony in a city in North America. Scientists believe they eat 10–30,000 pounds of insects every night!

12. In the 1790s, Lazzaro Spallanzani couldn't understand how bats hunted in the dark. And he wanted to find out

batly . . . um . . . badly. So, first, he blinded a group of bats. These bats were kept in a room with silk threads strung across. To his surprise, they could hunt easily without their eyes! They didn't bang into the walls of the room or get tangled in the silk threads even once! Next, he plugged their ears. Now they went about fumbling into the walls and threads. Spallanzani was happy—these bats could somehow see through their ears! It took scientists another hundred years to explain echolocation. And Spallanzani couldn't do more experiments with his bats because most of them died. Anybody would, with stitched eyes and plugged ears.

During World War I, war scientists made a device to find underwater submarines. This device was based on bats' use of echolocation.

13. Many bats drink water one drop at a time. They skim the water surface and get one drop of water in their jaws. Then they come again and get another drop of water. The bats keep doing this till they have had their fill. Are you thinking it takes them a whole afternoon to have a glass of water? No, they do it very quickly. For a long time, no one could make out how bats drank water because they were that quick. So, in the 1960s, a scientist called Webster took a thousand photographs per second of bats drinking water a drop at a time. (What if Webster took a thousand snaps *per hour* of us on a Sunday? He would find us sitting in the same position, watching TV.) Other bats, like fruit bats and flying foxes, wet themselves on the water's surface. They then sit and lick water from

WILD IN THE BACKYARD

their chest fur. So before you call your dad or your mum to give you a glass of water the next time, think about how much hard work bats have to do. Bat mothers feed their babies milk only for a few weeks. After that, the pups have to hunt and feed themselves.
14. You can put up a bat house in your garden. It would be pretty groovy to see the bats come out in the dark, cloaked in black, and fly away into the night. Do they go to meet the devil or to the land of the dead? Neither, really. They just fly away to eat insects, lizards and other such nourishing meals. The University of Florida has the largest man-made bat house in the world. Around 3 lakh bats have made it their home. Every night, these bats eat about 2.5 billion bugs!

BATTY BELIEFS

- Long, long ago, the Aztecs, Mayans and Zapotecs lived in South America. They were neighbouring cultures, and they all had some batty beliefs. The Aztecs believed that bats were creatures of the underworld. They came from the land of the dead.
- The Mayan ceramicists (those who make mud pots and pans) made bats appear as pop-eyed males. They also linked bats to humans due to some similarities in our skeletal structures.
- There is a legend that bats get caught in people's hair. You may have a swarm of mosquitoes dancing above your head. In that case, a hungry bat might dive down

to catch a few for supper. It has nothing to do with your hair. No, even if you have lice in your hair, it won't bother to pick them up.
- The Zapotecs carved bats on their burial urns. These bats had big claws and rounded ears. Do you know which other animals are associated with death? (Owls, scorpions and jaguars.)
- Templo Mayor, the 'Great Temple' of the Aztecs, has a life-size clay batman. The god of death. It has the body of a man but the head, hands and clawed feet of a bat.
- Some Mayan people believed that the bat was the devil's cook. It would come out at night from the underworld and collect the blood of animals to feed the devil.

Not all beliefs around bats are batty or deathly. In Poland and the Middle East, they consider bats lucky. A Chinese tale says bats are a symbol of happiness. They would surely make *us* happy if they ate that mighty eight-legged being that makes us yelp and jump out of our chairs like little Miss Muffet!

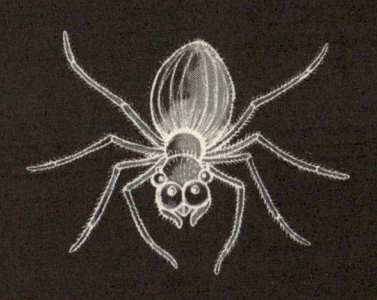

THE DREAMCATCHERS

They have four times the number of legs we have and make us yelp and dash out of their way all the time. If you do not want to come across one, you should go live in Antarctica. That is the only place on earth without . . . spiders! In the rest of the world, there are more than 40,000 of their kind.

What comes to mind when we talk of spiders are hairy tarantulas. They are TV stars and the largest spiders in the world. You see them crawling around (most of the time on TV, of course), with their hairy legs and dark eyes. And you shrink into your sofa as the supercool spider waves two of its bushy legs at you, saying howdy.

We leave the house for a few days and return to a tangle of cobwebs. Spiders have found cosy homes in our houses.

Spider: It's your home? Says who?

They hang about in our gardens, yards and backyards and, of course, in forests. The darn insects! Wait a minute. They are *not* insects. They are arachnids. And what on earth are arachnids? They sound like orchids but are nowhere close to being as pretty! They are the cousins of insects. While insects have antennae and six legs, arachnids have no antennae but eight legs.

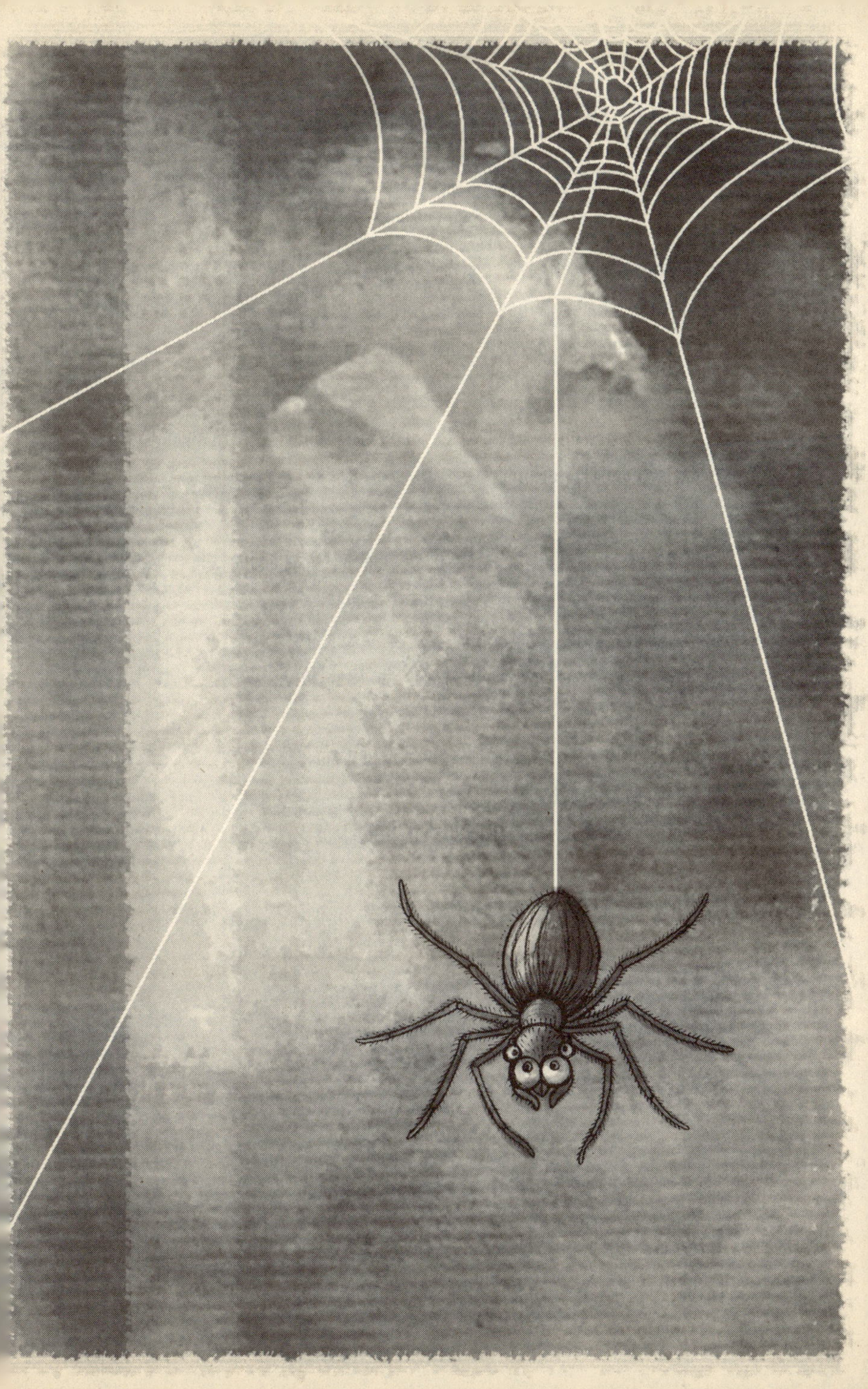

WILD IN THE BACKYARD

SUPER SPIDER STORIES (TRUE, OF COURSE)

Fill in the blanks with the word list you see below and you will be rewarded with some savage spider stories. If your score is between 8 and 10 you might be a close relative of Spider-Man!

> pesticides, cannibals, colonies, bristles, ghost, arachnophobia, beards, spinnerets, goliath, fishing

1. Spiders have _____ on their abdomens to produce silk.
2. The _____ is the world's biggest spider.
3. Bolas spiders are also called _____ spiders.
4. Spiders can have only liquid food. So they have _____ to filter the solid bits out.
5. Some spiders like tarantulas and baboon spiders have _____ that they throw at attackers.
6. Scientists are trying to develop harmless _____ from spider venom.
7. In 2011, many trees in Pakistan turned into _____ trees.
8. Many spiders prefer to live alone. But a few live in _____.
9. _____ is the unusual fear of spiders.
10. Some spiders, like black widows, are _____.

AREFA TEHSIN

ANSWERS

1. spinnerets

It is the organ that spins silk. Whenever you see tarantulas on the telly, you don't see them in their webs. They just trot about. It is because they do not build webs. In fact, many spiders don't. When we think of a web, we imagine an orb-like web that looks like a wheel. These webs are built only by a few kind of spiders called orb-web spiders. The rest of them just have tangles of webs (which we call cobwebs), web sheets, web ladders or no webs at all. Spiders use their silk in many ways:

- for wrapping their eggs
- as parachutes
- as safety ropes
- to lower themselves down from the ceiling and say hi to you

Hummingbirds use spider silk and sticks to make their nests. Spiders can fly like kites by releasing silk. They do this to travel from one place to another. Helium balloons flying at great heights to collect air samples have come across travelling spiders!

Some people weave threads in the shape of spider webs and hang them from their beds. This is called a dreamcatcher and is supposed to catch, well, your dreams. Now, if the dream was about your history test and not you flying with a cape, tough luck!

2. goliath

It is a kind of tarantula that eats toads, birds, lizards, insects and even snakes! Except for one kind of spider, the *Bagheera kipling* that eats vegetable matter, all the other 40,000-plus spiders are carnivorous. They generally catch and eat crisp and juicy insects and even other spiders. And they use their sticky webs to catch their prey. After all, for its weight, spider's silk is tougher than steel!

Even bats get caught in big spiderwebs! And the spider itself can be much smaller than the bat—it seals the bat's face first to avoid a bat bite. Then it seals the rest of the bat's body. And then it kills the bat with a hundred bites!

3. fishing

Some spiders use ways other than sticky webs to catch their prey. The bolas spider throws a sticky blob of silk to catch flies and moths. It is just like a fisherman catching fish with his fishing rod. Then there are net-casting spiders, like the ogre-faced spider. But the more interesting ones are the water spiders. They live their lives within 'diving bell' webs. If their prey touches the bell, they dart out and catch it.

Water spider: Welcome home, munchkins!

4. beards

Spiders have fangs to inject venom, but no jaws. So they filter their food and have only liquids. Guess what—spider poo is not mucky but always solid! Haven't you always wondered what spider poo looked like?

They have other interesting features too. Most spiders have eight eyes. Some, though, have less and some more. The ones who live in caves have no eyes at all. Have you ever wondered why a dead spider's legs curl up? It's because they use liquid pressure in their bodies to spread their legs when they're alive. The jumping spiders can increase the blood pressure in their back four legs to eight times the normal pressure. That is why they can jump fifty times their length! With legs like these, who'd want to cycle to school?

5. bristles

Yes, these spiders have bristles or 'irritating hair' on their bodies. They can throw these bristles at anyone who tries to attack them. The bristles stick to the attacker's skin or eyes, causing great irritation. No wonder they're called 'irritating hair'!

Tarantulas are cooked and eaten in Cambodia and other countries. The cooks remove these bristles first. What if a cook forgets to remove the bristles before cooking a crispy tarantula? Well, that is a question to crunch on.

6. pesticides

Okay, now think about this. Spiders use their venom to kill insects. Most of their venom is harmless to us. What if we made a lot of spider venom? We could use it to kill insects on farms. And it would not be as harmful to use as the pesticides we use today. Now isn't that a smart idea?

Scientists have not stopped there. They are trying to make spider silk too. Why? Well, because spider silk is light and super strong. How, you ask? Ah, now that's a strange one—with goat's milk and plant leaves!

7. ghost

In the July of 2010, there were severe floods in Pakistan. The waters did not recede till the following year. To avoid drowning, millions of spiders climbed up trees in the Sindh Province. There, they built their webs, which covered the trees like ghostly cloaks. These ghost trees were good for the locals, as spiders ate away a lot of mosquitoes, reducing the risk of malaria. You can check their snaps on the Internet, of course.

8. colonies

Some kinds of spiders prefer to live together, and thousands of them can live in a single colony! They do not have complex families like ants do. Spiders just share food and defend their eggs together. And protect their food from thieves.

Mama spiders carry their eggs in fancy silk sacs. One mama spider can lay up to 3000 eggs! With some kinds of spiders, like many of the orb-weavers, the mama dies after laying eggs. Other lady-spiders protect these orphan egg sacs.

They hide them in their nests or attach them to their webs or drag them along with them.

The spiderlings have to be on their own once they hatch. But some spiderlings are difficult to get rid of. The wolf spider carries her little ones on her back. They cling to her bristles and take a free ride everywhere. Some mamas are soft-hearted and give in to the spiderlings' begging, and hand over their prey to them.

Mama Spider: Aww . . . okay, kiddies. Scrunch up my dead beetle.

9. arachnophobia

Remember spiders are arachnids? And phobia means fear.

Symptoms of arachnophobia:

- seeing a web and throwing a fit
- seeing a web and screaming and crying
- seeing a web and breaking into a sweat
- knees turning to jelly upon seeing a picture of a spider

Though people get jittery when you cry 'spider!', death by spider bite is very, very rare. Around a hundred people died due to spider bite in the last century. That means one death in the world per year. Ever wondered how many people die due to car accidents? One person every twenty-five seconds!

The world's most dangerous spiders are funnel-web spiders. Recluse spiders, Brazilian wandering spiders and widow spiders also have rather nasty bites. And they bite only in self-defence. Most spider bites are not any worse than a mosquito bite. Your baby brother biting you can be much more painful.

10. cannibals (those who eat their own kind)

Oh yes, these widows and some other kinds of spiders, like the Australian redback spider, may kill their boyfriends and even eat them! The guy is both the girl's date and dinner. The angry ladies are much bigger in size than the gents. The gent of one kind of tangle-web spider is just 1 per cent the size of the lady! But she is a gentle giant and doesn't eat her mate. Or maybe he is just not worth eating. Those who are worth eating try hard to get away from the lady after the date and many of them manage to escape.

Boyfriend: Darling . . . I never called you fat! Honest . . .

Most spiders don't live more than two years. There are a few, including tarantulas, who can live up to twenty-five years in a zoo or a cage. (It is called living in captivity. Or being captive. It means not being free. It's like not being able to run away from home or school. Do you feel the same?)

Did you know . . .

Some kinds of spiderlings eat their mamas after they're born. Now that's really the height of being hungry!

Before you go to your friends and say—'Oh my god, did you know that some baby spiders eat their nagging mums?'—wait. You might have another cool neighbour you'd like to read and talk about. And this one can munch on a snake for supper.

THE SERPENT HUNTERS

No, the mongoose is not a goose. It was called *mungus* in Marathi. Then the English added the 'goose' to it and named it mongoose. It is not your regular annoying neighbour who has to make his presence felt by honking his car or playing loud music. The mongoose is bold but shy and visits our backyards and lanes only sometimes. If you're lucky, you can spot it crossing an undisturbed road or dashing across your backyard.

The Indian grey mongoose or *Nevlaa* is what we most commonly see in our homes. We need a lot of trees and plants for the wild in our backyard to live happily. Ask your mum and dad to plant as many trees in your garden and out in your lane as possible.

Mainly found in South Asia, Africa and south Europe, the mongoose is a meat-eating mammal. It eats insects and birds, crabs and earthworms, rats and eggs, and even anything that's dead. Just basically whatever it can lay its paws on. It is not picky, as your parents think you are! It has a sleek body, a long face, rounded ears and a long tail that narrows at the end, and its brown or grey grizzled fur makes it look as if it has just woken up. A few of the twenty-nine different kinds of mongooses have rings or stripes on their tails. What, you thought only you wore stylish patterns on your T-shirts and shorts?

I bet you're itching to know how the mongoose is a snake hunter. Let's solve the given mongoose quiz and find out the answer.

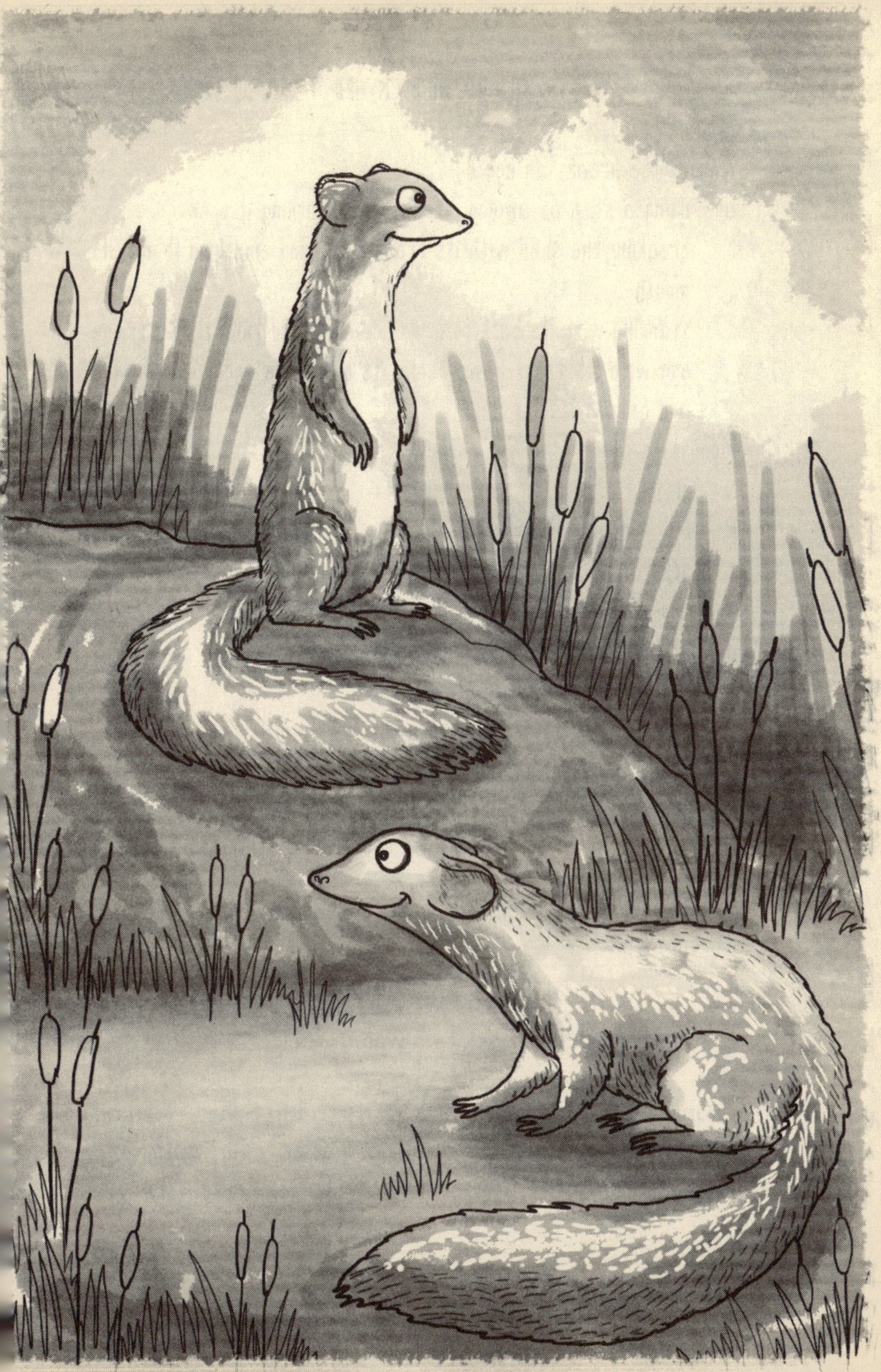

WILD IN THE BACKYARD

1. A mongoose breaks an egg by:
   a. using a stick as an egg cracker and cracking it open
   b. breaking the shell with its front paws and emptying it into its mouth
   c. standing with its back to a wall or rock, and then throwing the egg with its front paws below its body. The egg hits the wall and breaks.
2. Mongooses
   a. giggle
   b. LOL (Laugh Out Loud)
   c. snigger
3. Which god carries a mongoose?
   a. Athena (the Greek goddess of wisdom)
   b. Kubera (the Hindu god of wealth)
   c. Mictlantecuhtli (the Aztec god of the dead)
4. Which country does not allow mongooses?
   a. Sri Lanka
   b. Egypt
   c. the US

ANSWERS

1. c. standing with its back to a wall or rock

The mongoose is a posh hunter with a great sense of smell and sight. The Indian grey mongoose even eats scorpions. And yes, mongooses hunt and eat snakes too! Snakes are one of their favourite foods, be it the infamous black mambas or the cobras! It is not just the mongooses' good looks, thick coats and quick movements that do the trick. The venom of some snakes, including cobras, does not affect mongooses! Cobras are not ones to take it lying down, though. They put up a fierce struggle. A mongoose generally breaks a cobra's neck. No need to have nightmares about mongooses now! They don't attack humans like they attack snakes. They know who the nastier of the two is, and keep away from us.

There are three other mammals on whom the venom of a cobra and some other snakes does not work:

- honey badgers
- hedgehogs
- pigs

Pig: Hah! And you thought we were thick-skinned, thickheaded and dirty. To be used as piggy banks and eaten as pork chops. We'll see who runs away on seeing a cobra!

2. a. giggle

Mongooses make a high-pitched giggling sound when they find a date. Anyone would be happy finding a date, don't you think?

Many kinds of mongooses are happy living alone all their lives. Only once in a while do they go out on a date with their mate. There are some mongooses who live and travel in groups. Most mongooses live on land. However, a few prefer a fancier lifestyle with a nice pool of water close by. And some others prefer cool treetop homes.

3. b. Kubera

The calm Athena is associated with owls. The blood-spattered, skeleton-like Mictlantecuhtli is linked to owls, bats and spiders. The pot-bellied Kubera, the Hindu god of wealth, often holds a mongoose in his hands. Maybe to show his victory over the nagas—the snakes. The mongoose he holds is a golden one that spits out gems. Wouldn't you like to have one such? Take my word, plain round pebbles are better and much more fun to play with.

4. c. the US

Except Hawaii, none of the other states in the US allow mongooses. They were once brought into West Indies to kill rats. They ended up killing and eating many other small animals. The ones who got the mongooses in had not read this chapter. Otherwise, they would have known, like you, that mongooses are not fussy about what they eat. Even in the many places mongooses are found, they have become quite scarce. Because of humans, of course. We just destroy their homes and build our own. You can ban mongooses from coming in, but how do you ban humans?

Mongooses belong to the same family as meerkats. They're cousins of hyenas, civets and cats. Except for the meerkats, no other kind of mongoose can be brought into New Zealand either.

MR MAGOO'S STORY

The US made an exception for Mr Magoo. He was a well-mannered, tea-sipping mongoose. A seaman brought him to the US in the 1960s, and the officials came to know about him living in the Duluth Zoo. And though he was quite famous by then, it still was not legal for him to live in the US. So Mr Magoo was given the death sentence. But then, people got real hot at this and demanded that he live. And so he was saved and continued to be one of the most popular animals at the Duluth Zoo. Fame was Mr Magoo's key to life!

Some people keep mongooses as pets, and in some countries, they are also trained to mock-fight snakes. The Indian grey mongoose, among others, is the most popular choice for this purpose. Some snake charmers even keep mongooses with them to have mock fights between the two arch-enemies to entertain people.

Speaking of snakes, there might be one right inside your flowerpot!

BLISSFULLY BLIND

In your garden, beneath the layers of mud, live creatures big and small. These creatures of the shadows live underground—sometimes under our feet! They slither noiselessly, surfacing above the ground at times to take a peek at the world and then disappearing into the dark again. And here's the thing—some of them are blind. What would you see with mud and sludge all around you, anyway?

We are talking about a blind snake, *and* a Brahminy at that! Brahminy is the Latin word for Brahmin. Way back, saints, who were mostly Brahmin, wore clothes that were *geruwa* (ochre) coloured. And some lazy wise guy named all creatures of a similar colour Brahminy. The critters thus named have fur, feather or hide, all of the same colour. For example, the Brahminy mynah, Brahminy kite, Brahminy sea turtle, and the Brahminy duck.

SAVVY SNAKES

Brahminy snakes are garden savvy. If the temperature and humidity (that's the amount of water vapour in the air) are right for living underground, you'll find, more often than not, that you have a blind neighbour—yes, a snake. Now let's not quiver over the S word. Snakes are not lying in wait in the garden to bite your little toe with their fangs as you pass by. No, they are not ambush assassins. Why would they waste their precious venom on us—we're not even their meal! Unless they're dumb. And that they're not. They only attack and bite when they feel they may be in danger.

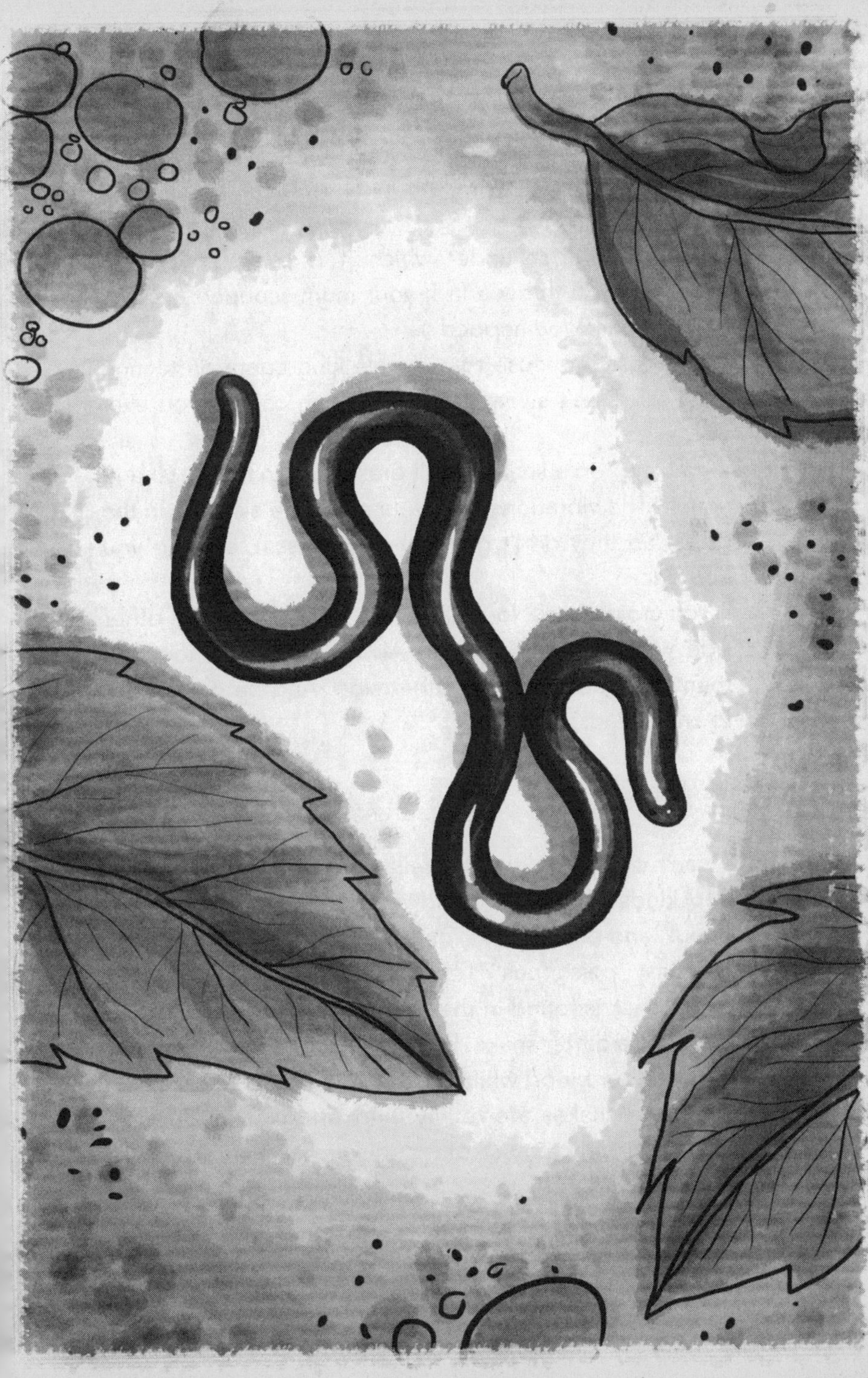

Times when a snake may feel it's in danger:

- if you lift a rock under which it is cosily coiled up. (Wouldn't you throw a fit if your mum scooped up your blanket while you napped?)
- if you pass too close to a female king cobra protecting her nest. Don't sweat. There is a slim chance you ever will.
- if you step on a snake in tall grass—it can't see you and you, it. The vibrations from your steps are also less in the grass. So they don't get a chance to scat, sensing you approach.
- if you cross over a log and place your feet on the other side without checking first. Always climb the log and then jump down on the other side. And be careful not to crash-land!

DON'T POISON MY MIND!

How many of these slithering fellas are poisonous? Out of the 216 kinds of snakes found in India, only fifty-two are poisonous, and out of these, only five are deadly poisonous. Did I just say 'poisonous'? I beg your pardon. There are no poisonous snakes found in the world! Except two—a kind of keelback and a garter snake. Snakes are venomous. Venom is injected into our blood while poison is usually eaten.

The blind snakes are totally harmless. Not at all glitzy or nerve-racking like most other snakes. All that slithers is not bold! They blend into the surroundings with their earthy colours of brown and pink. Due to their colour, shape and size, they are often mistaken for earthworms. Think it's funny to look like an earthworm? It's smart, actually. You might have come across earthworms time and again but not noticed them. What if you'd known it was a snake? You'd have squawked, run away or maybe beaten it to a pulp, sending it right to snake heaven!

BLIND BRAHMINY

The Brahminy blind snake is, well, blind. Its eyes are covered in scales. The scales are like frosted glass. You can't see through them but they let light pass through. So the snake can't see but can detect how strong or weak the light is. The adults are 2–6 in. long, without any narrowing at the neck like most other snakes. They are the same size throughout. This means you can't see a head and can't tell one end from the other. These snakes look just like earthworms.

How do you know which is which? Earthworms move very slowly, bending and straightening their bodies, while blind snakes slither past with speed. And, blind snakes do not have segments like earthworms. That is, they have a smooth body and don't look like lumps put together. You can't figure out head or tail of this snake!

My head has no eyes,
I live in the scum.
The earthworm's my size
And my tail has no bum.

Their favourite places to live are mounds of ants and termites. But they are far from being thankful lodgers. They feed on their hosts' eggs, larvae and pupae.

NO LADS, ONLY LADIES

The blind snake is also called the 'flowerpot snake'. Although it is found in Asia and Africa, it was spread to various parts of the world through the trading of plants, which gave it this name. A snake in your flowerpot—now won't that be cool! If your mum finds you admiring it in the garden and freaks out shouting, 'Get away, he'll bite!' just tell her smugly what you have learnt about them. None of the blind snakes is a 'he'. They are all ladies! Blind snakes do not need a daddy to be born. An 'embryo'—a developing baby snake—comes into being without any fertilization.

And bite? No, these ladies don't engage in such uncivilized activities. There are enough mosquitoes around to do the job.

OH, THEM BLOODSUCKERS!

If they drink your blood, you won't become a vampire. But they may leave you, at best, itching, and at worst, drooling and feverish in your beds. Those little Draculas—mosquitoes! They fly straight from drains and sewers to buzz in your ear and feast on your blood.

The word 'mosquito' has fancy Spanish origins and means 'little fly'. And little flies they are. There are no less than 3500 kinds of them the world over! Mosquitoes are found in the mountains, at the seashore and everywhere in-between—

- inside our houses
- outside our houses
- in the cities
- in the jungles

BLOOD RELATIONS

Found everywhere except Antarctica, mosquitoes don't feed on blood for themselves. The blood is for them to produce a healthy number of eggs and keep them nourished. As for their own diet, they depend on the nectar from flowers, just like their distant cousins. Do you know who the cousins of these awful mosquitoes are? The stylish butterflies! Both are insects, after all.

NO DEADLY DANDIES

They are not as harmless as the leeches that suck your blood and fall off when their bellies are full; they spread some of

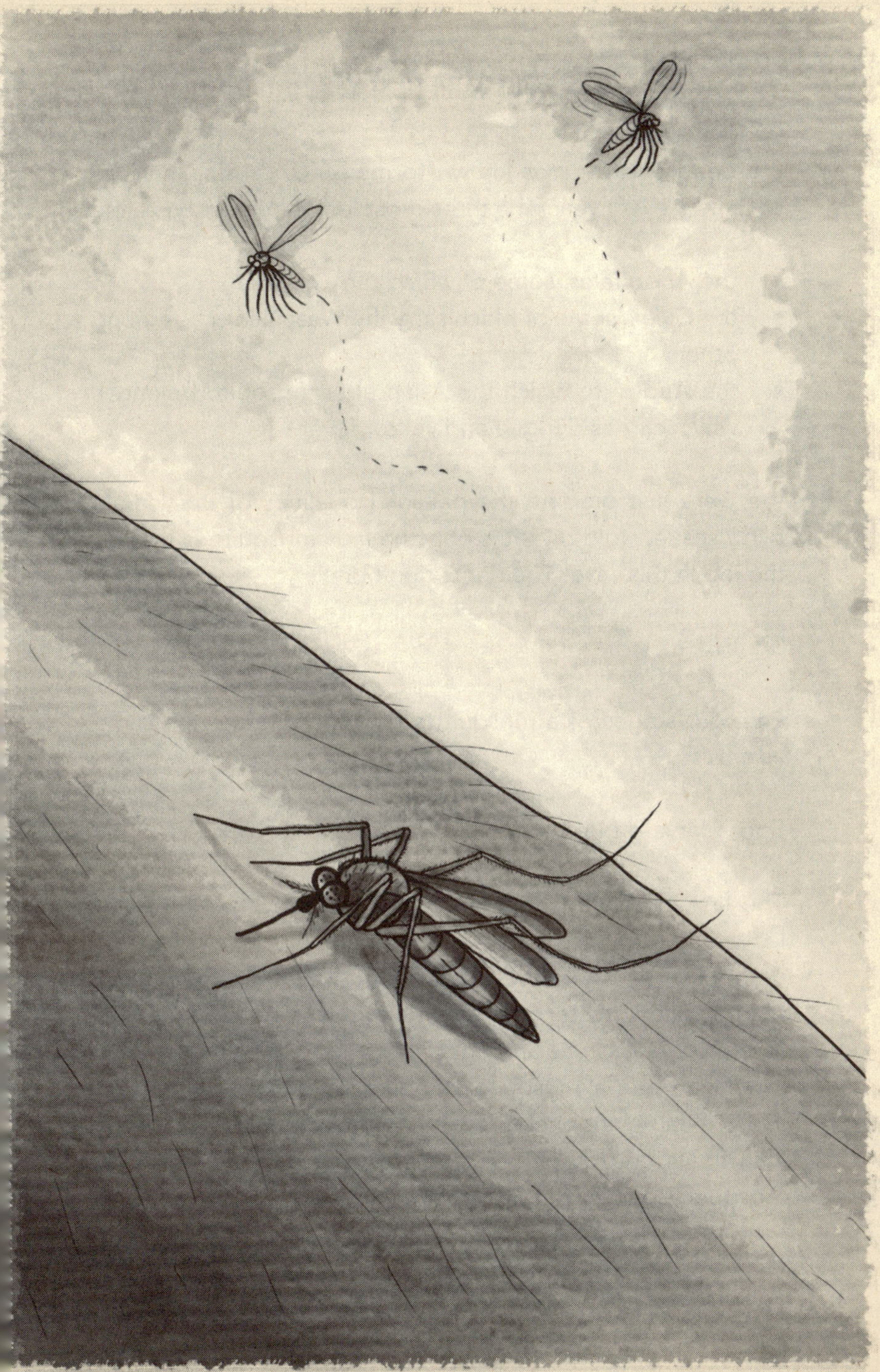

the deadliest diseases known to mankind, causing millions of deaths every year. The three most lethal mosquitoes are:

- the *Anopheles,* some of which carry malaria
- the *Culex,* some of which carry the West Nile virus among others
- the *Aedes* (to which the Asian tiger mosquito belongs), which carries dengue and yellow fever

We were just praising the peaceful qualities of the female blind snake. Hold on—it is only the lady mosquitoes that do the job in this case! The gents don't bite.

GIRL POWER

The four stages of a mosquito's growth cycle are the same as a fly's.

Egg→ larva→ pupa→ adult

The first three stages need still water to develop. So don't leave any puddles or damp vessels around your garden or home, like empty bottles. If there is a little pond you need to keep filled, pester your parents to put some fish in it. Fish love mosquito larvae and eggs.

If you see a mosquito bobbing over water, it is most likely a lady anopheles dropping her cigar-shaped eggs with floats one by one. A single female of many common mosquito species can lay around 200 eggs at a time. Over a period of weeks, one breeding pair of mosquitoes can produce thousands of them! Have you ever had a swarm of mosquitoes over your head in the evenings? The guys form these swarms and the girls fly inside these swarms, looking out for the coolest boys. The males of all mosquito species have bushier antennae. And do you know what for? To detect the typical whine of the females! Now don't say you aren't surprised. That's one heck of a party happening above your head!

SCRATCH, SCRATCH...

God! That annoying itch . . . when a mosquito lands on you and takes a mouthful of your blood! Mosquitoes, too, have their likes and dislikes, you know. Are you one of those the mosquitoes swarm towards when you're in a group?

That may be because:

- you have type O blood (there are eight blood types)
- you're a heavy breather
- your body is warmer than the others'
- or, *ahem*, you have a lot of skin bacteria (um . . . tough call—bath or mosquito bite?)

Mosquitoes are also attracted to pregnant women. The good news is that they prefer cattle, birds and horses to humans. Wise choice, that. The bad news is, global warming and increasing temperatures will make it easy for them to survive in more and more places. (Remember they like warm places?) And at the same time, the rising temperatures will decrease their predators. Some of their predators are frogs, birds, bats and dragonflies, among others. Have you ever dreamed of flying a spaceship and slaying some aliens? Let's start with swatting a mosquito first.

Don't be disheartened if you can't swat one. Who knows, some other species in the future might extract our DNA from a mosquito's belly, like they did in *Jurassic Park,* and bring our species back to life!

Ah, those 'terrible lizards' of the Jurassic era! We have a few lizards in our backyard too, though a wee bit less terrible. Let's check them out.

MORE BLOODSUCKERS

Well, these are bloodsuckers too! But only in name. The garden lizard or *Calotes* can change the colour of its head and its neck from light brownish-olive to blood red. The he-lizard does this at times when he has to look smart for the gals. Ugh, who'd want that? But wait, he gets red with anger too. Picture it: your head turning from wheat brown to flaming red when your teacher fails you in the history test. Or when your mum tells you to stop playing and finish your homework. Hmm . . . would it scare away your teacher or your mum? Probably not! Instead, you might earn the name bloodsucker too. And don't tell me you're called that already!

BLOOD RELATIONS

Yes, all lizards are related to dinosaurs—more or less. But if we take a closer peek, our very own backyard bloodsuckers are closely related to iguanas, though iguanas are only found in the New World, i.e. the Americas. You're probably wondering, 'Are we old or what?' The people from Europe thought we were. Vasco de Gama had 'discovered' us long before Columbus 'discovered' America. And so, before the sixteenth century, before the Europeans landed in America, they thought the world consisted only of Europe, Africa and Asia. So these three are now together called the Old World. And that includes us oldies.

Our backyard bloodsuckers' close kin, iguanas from the New World, are no less terrible looking than the 'terrible lizards'—the dinosaurs.

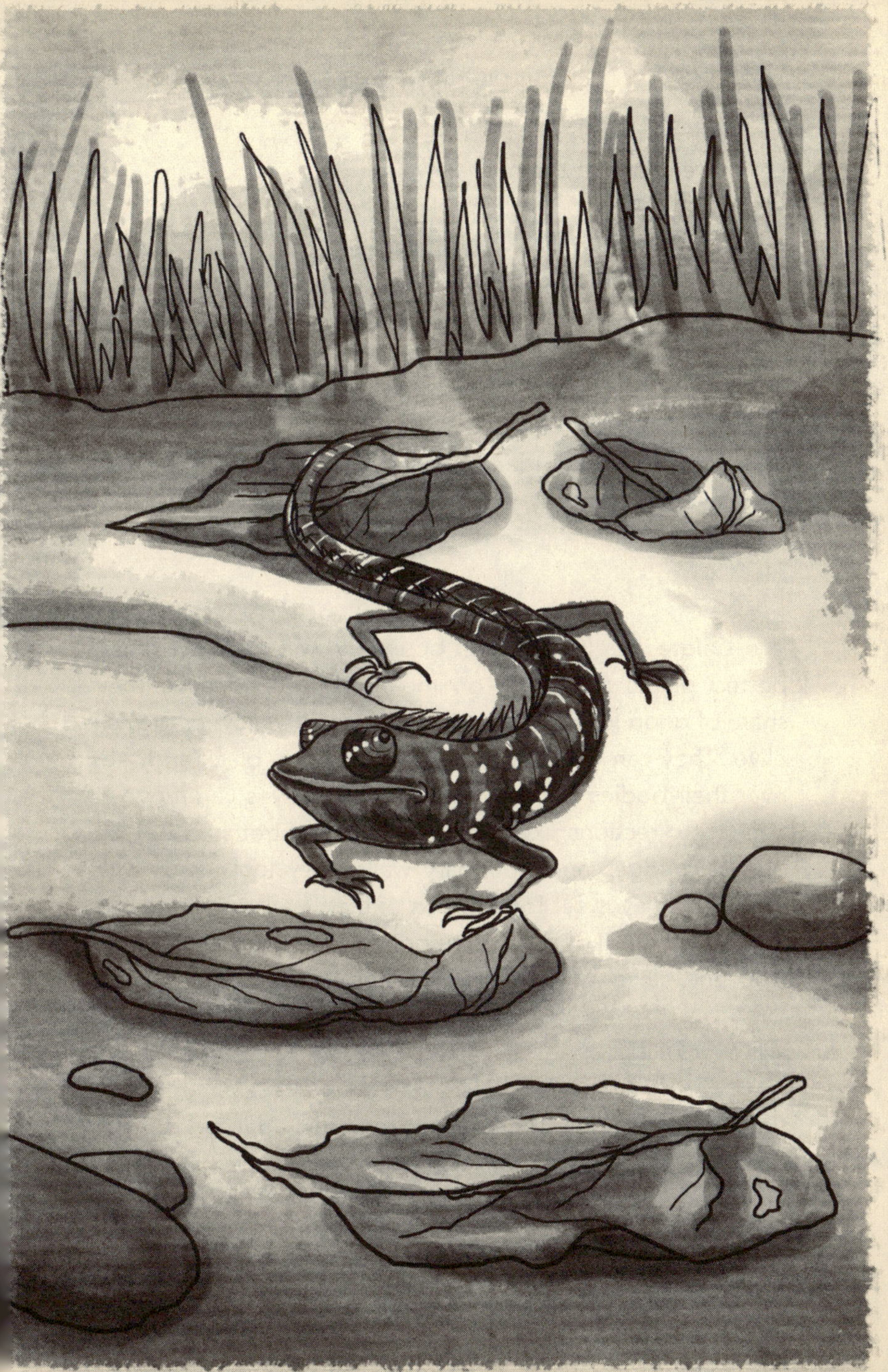

WILD IN THE BACKYARD

Let's take a look at them, shall we?

- rod-like upright scales on their heads
- spines running right down their backs to their tails
- a third eye (not quite unlike Shiva's) in the middle of their heads
- a shield-like round scale on their cheek

There! You have your iguana. What wouldn't we give for such fearsome features!

BLOODY LOOKS

The *Calotes* strolling on our boundary walls, garden grass, potted plants and trees on the roadside also have their share of good looks. They can be brownish yellow or greyish olive. They can change their colour to deep black and red, over their bodies and pointed tails. Their eyes can move in different directions like the chameleons'. Stretched out on bushes, hedges and boundary walls, they look at us with their sleepy eyes set to the sides of their leathery heads and probably think, 'Look who's struggling with homework, house work and office work. And they call *us* leather heads?'

WHAT'S FOR DINNER?

Calotes or garden lizards have smartly adapted to our gardens. They shed their skin once in a while, like other reptiles, and get brand new skin. Their favourite foods are insects and other small animals, including lizards. Sometimes, they eat vegetable matter too. Their silent, sleepy expression doesn't change while gulping down vegetables, though. My guess is that they don't enjoy the vegetables much. Their sleepiness is gone in a jiffy, however, when they attack and catch an unsuspecting grasshopper or a small rodent in their jaws. Although they have a sharp set of teeth, they can't tear prey with it. They must swallow it whole, so they stun the prey by shaking it with jerks. Measuring around 37 cm from head to tail, *Calotes* are hard-nosed hunters. Their motto: if you can't tear them, shake them! Sometimes, a young hunter might choke to death by swallowing prey too big for her size. Size matters, it would seem.

I BRING YOU A RED, RED ROSE ... UM ... THROAT

In the summer, their dating and mating season, the males change to bright red. Generally, the red is more around the throat, but it can be over the head or all over the body and tail like a red, patchy Superman costume. The stud in love puffs up his throat, bringing the girl's attention to his super-lizard red head, eyeing her sideways. The boys compete with each over who's more regular with exercise, and even go to the extent of doing push-ups to show off their strength and scare away the other boys from their territory! If the girl is impressed by a boy's flashy, inflated throat and all the promises he makes, she agrees to be his mate. Just for a season, mind you. And why just a season, you ask? Well, it's not like the good-for-nothing, half-red super lizard stays back after the date to find her a safe place to lay the eggs!

The eggs are spindle-shaped and spongy and leathery to touch. They are laid in a dug-up hole, ten to twenty at a time, and covered in moist soil. The eggs hatch long after both the respectable parents have taken off. The adults can grow up to be 37 cm long from snout to tail, provided they get enough to eat (without their mums and dads feeding them) as they grow up. And of course, if they can avoid being eaten by other animals. *Calotes* even play dead to avoid hunters.

MS AND MR AGAMID

There are twenty-seven different kinds of *Calotes*. They belong to the Agamid family of lizards. Like you may belong to the Akhtar or Acharya or Adani or Agarwal or Aguiar family of humans. Yes, yes, there are many, many other human families too. But where there are fewer humans, like in the forests of the Western Ghats or northeast India, there are more Agamids.

After a rain shower, you should look at these bloodsuckers come down to the ground and eat the insects freshly fallen from the trees. And who knows, a house crow may just swoop down, pick up the happily eating bloodsucker and fly away. Life is not all red—er . . . I mean rosy—after all.

CRAFTY CROWS

They might not look as dandy as peacocks or sing sweet nothings like koels, but they're brave, scary-looking and brainy. Be it the frightful crow shown with the boy-devil Damien in *The Omen* or the smart, pebble-dropping crow in Aesop's fable, crows carry themselves with a devil-may-care attitude.

There are many kinds of crows found all over the globe. The house crow, as the name suggests, is most widely found near houses in villages and cities. The scientific name of our house crow is *Corvus splendens*, which means 'shining raven'. It wears a grey neck-collar over its black robes and is found in and around human settlements. As our numbers have exploded, so have those of house crows. Singapore alone recorded a population density of 190 crows per sq. km in 2001!

Although the house crow is from Asia, it hopped on to ships and, like Columbus, discovered many new lands (like Africa, Europe and the Middle East), where it is now well-settled. It eats just about everything that can be eaten, and that is what makes it such a great survivor. (That means it's a toughie!)

In the list given below, can you tell which is the one thing crows don't eat?

- scraps from garbage dumps
- grains
- fruit
- insects
- birds' eggs
- reptiles
- baby squirrels

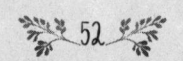

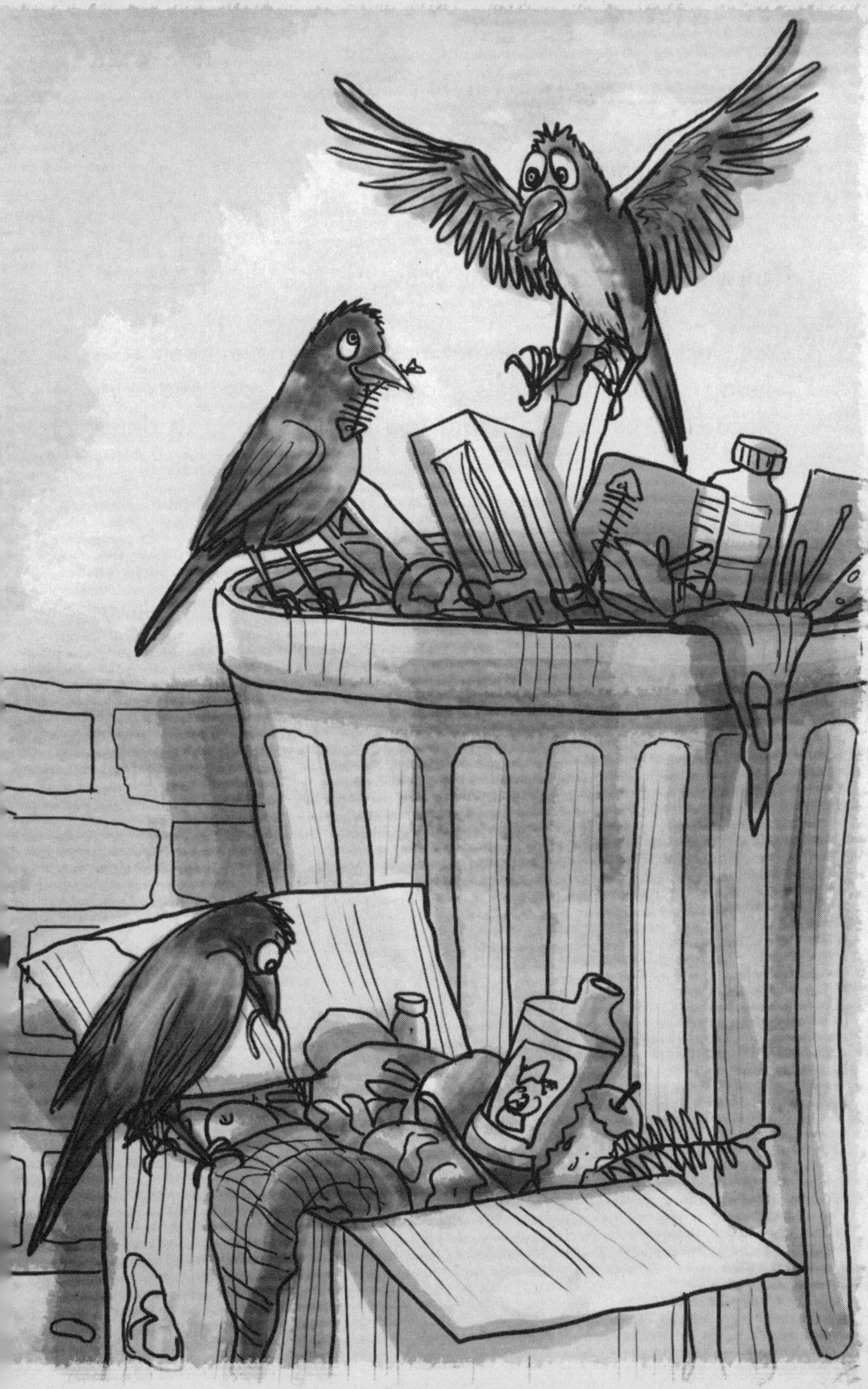

- dead animals
- sand

Answer: Crows eat all of the above.

Yes, including sand! Sometimes, crows have been seen eating sand after meals. Some other birds, and even crocodiles, eat sand. Before you ask why—it is to digest food better by grinding it with sand in their stomachs. No wonder! After eating all this rubbish, one would need stones to grind it.

They make their untidy stick nests (even using metal wires if they can get them from the garbage) mainly in large trees with big crowns. Sometimes even on telephone poles and building ledges. The birdman of India, Dr Salim Ali, even found a plier in one nest! They prefer to live together like us, and you can see them nesting and roosting together. They like living in trees found around busy streets, markets and buildings—isn't it smart of them to be near their food source at all times! And they make great use of human resources. Use humans for a change, what an idea!

DON'T PECK ME!

The ever-hopping, alert and wary crows are considered a pain in the lands they've introduced themselves. They peck on and damage crops and steal grain. They have been known to go for free rides on buffaloes and other cattle to pick off their ticks. 'What's wrong with that?' you'll ask. But wait! They don't stop at that. An open sore of a living animal within reach? They'll peck at that too. Nice of them.

Their flock is called a 'murder' and their noisy *kaaa-kaaa* call is not exactly that of an epic songster. But yes, crows do us a great service—scavenging. It means eating the dead and the wasted. Since vultures were almost wiped out from India, crows have remained some of the main scavengers (those who eat refuse and dead meat) in towns and villages. Since we're too lazy to clear our own waste, any help is welcome.

If the eagle is the gentleman, the crow is the bad guy. Wait. Do you know the sweet-talking koel lays her eggs in the crow's nest? The koel couple doesn't request to rent the nest. The lad and the lass fight with the crow to forcefully lay their eggs in its nest. Or else, they slyly sneak into the nest, kicking the crow's eggs down the tree and laying their own eggs in their place. The ma and pa crows feed and fend for the koels' chicks, believing them to be their own little ones. So who's the bad guy, huh?

MAD MYTHS

There are many crazy crow-related myths and beliefs doing the rounds all around the world. Not just the house crow, but all the different kinds of crows belonging to the *Corvus* gang. Yeah, I know. It sounds like the Italian mafia!

- Sweden: Ravens (a kind of black, scary crow) are ghosts of murdered men.
- Ireland: Crows are linked with Morrigon, the goddess of war and death.

- Australia: Aboriginals, the natives of Australia, believe crows are tricksters and that they have the souls of their ancestors.
- China: According to their mythology, the world originally had ten suns, carried by ten crows. (No wonder crows are so tanned!)

The list of crazy crow-related beliefs in various countries and cultures is a long one. Back home, they say that if a crow sits on your terrace and caws, you're expected to have guests. Good, timely warning, in case you want to scat before they arrive!

CLEVER CROW

'Oh, he's a birdbrain!' we say. Birds are not smart. They may be chic dancers, swanky fliers, posh hunters, world travellers and sweet singers, but smart? Nah.

Yeah, crows are among the smartest non-human animals. They come and drop the nuts they're carrying at traffic signals so that the cars passing by can break the nuts' hard shells. They have super memory and use various tools to solve problems. Recently, a few scientists in Auckland decided to try out the thirsty-crow story in their lab. Remember the story of the crow dropping pebbles in the pitcher to raise the level of the water? The result of the experiments points out that crows are as clever with some tasks as human seven-year-olds! So tell me, are you as smart as a crow?

Crows, it turns out, are super smart and super survivors too. But hey, this scurrying icky little being in your home, constantly flicking its two antennae, is an ultra-super survivor. Let's see who it is!

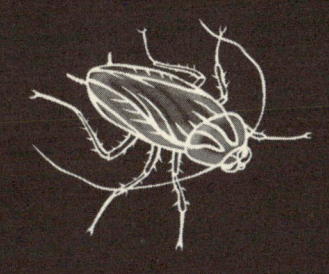

THE SUPER SURVIVORS

A hiss in the dark . . . you switch on the light of your bathroom and lo! It comes flying at you! Or it just dashes down the drain, flattening its chocolate brown body into a thin gap. You can maybe just get a glimpse of its thorny legs before it disappears into the dark depths of the pipeline. Yes, it is the mighty cockroach.

Big and small. In your kitchen and your bathroom. Sharing your home. Living all around you. The ones you see are only a few—there might well be up to 20,000 of them living in your house!

MEET THE ROACHES

Cockroaches live in most places of the world. Their great, great . . . greatest grandmom and granddad roachoids existed 295 million years ago!

Fun family facts

1. There are around 4600 kinds of cockroaches found all over the world!
2. Don't flinch. All cockroaches are not pests. Only around 30 of the 4600 live with humans in their homes. The ancient cockroaches were not as big as the dinosaurs. They were, in fact, smaller than the biggest cockroaches found today.
3. The cockroaches' closest relatives are termites and praying mantises.

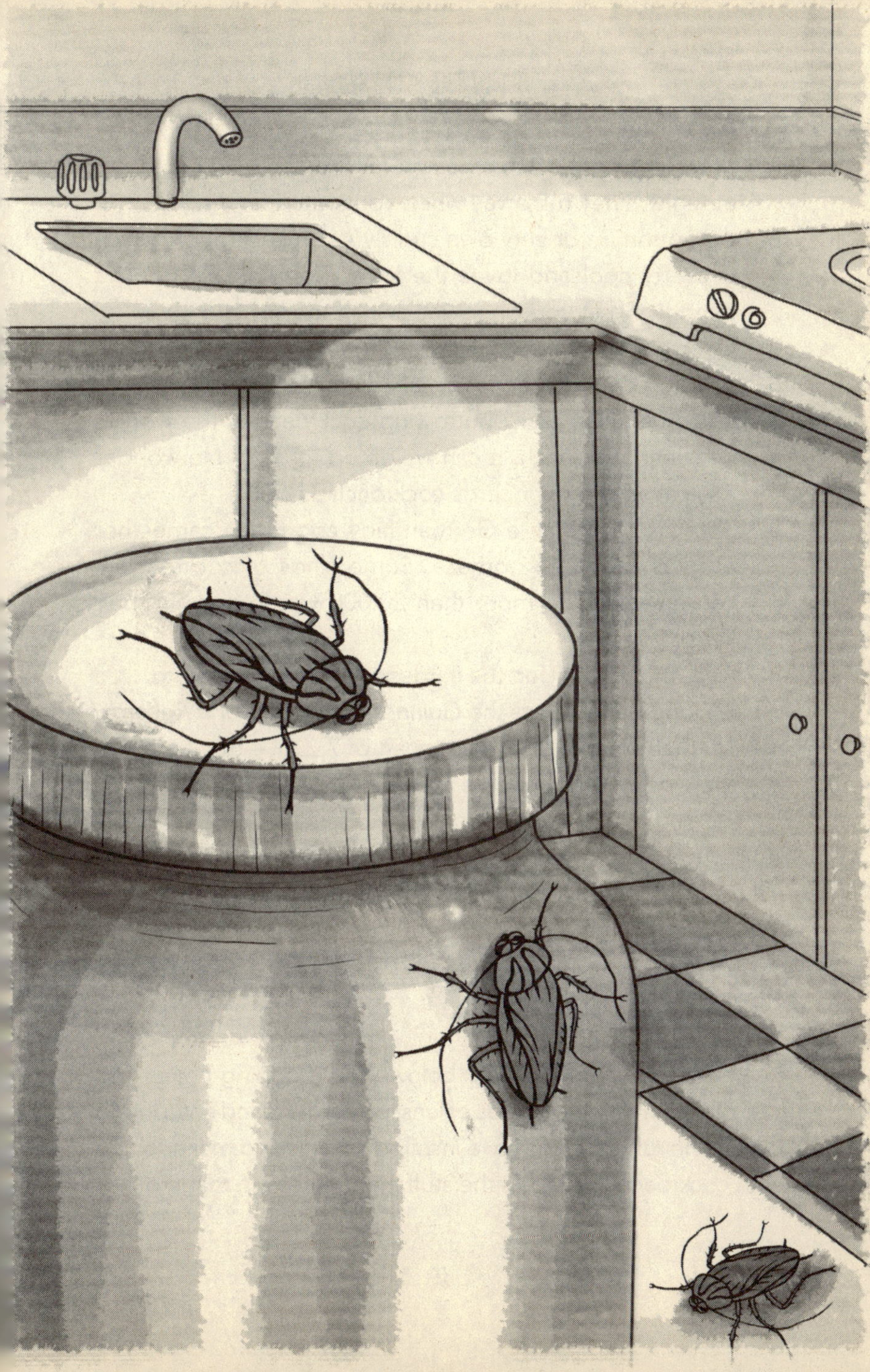

WILD IN THE BACKYARD

4. Most kinds of cockroaches prefer the dark and come out at night. They run away when you switch on the light. An exception is our very own cuddly Asian cockroach, which is pretty cool and loves the light. That's why it doesn't mind flying at you when you switch the lights on.
5. Cockroaches prefer to live with friends and family.
6. A group of cockroaches is called an intrusion.
7. The Australian giant burrowing cockroach is the world's heaviest cockroach. It can weigh up to 30 g! No wonder it is called the rhinoceros cockroach as well.
8. The case in which a German lady cockroach carries her eggs is called an ootheca. Some kinds of cockroaches can give birth to more than 20,000 young ones in their lives!
9. And the award for the largest cockroach goes to . . . *M. longipennis*! Says the *Guinness Book of World Records*.
10. *M. Blaberoides* has a wingspan of 7.2 in.—the largest in the world. Now imagine *that* flying at you!

And why do they have these long, confusing names, anyway? Why can't they just be called the dino roach or the horror cockro? Beats me!

THE VILLAINS WITH TWO ANTENNAE . . .

. . . have their chewing gear below their drooping heads and two big eyes with thousands of lenses (they're called compound eyes). Their thorny legs have inspired scientists to make robots with cockroach-like legs—the stuff nightmares are made of.

The four most popular pests are the Asian cockroach, the American cockroach, the German cockroach and the Oriental cockroach. These pest cockroaches love warm places like drains and garbage pits in buildings. No wonder cockroaches found in the tropics are bigger than their cousins found in colder countries. They spread diseases and cause allergies in humans. And they can leave an awfully bad smell too! They can eat almost anything, including the toothpaste left on your toothbrush. Argh! Do make sure you wash it properly before you use it. Who knows what nibbles on it at night . . . When push comes to shove, they can eat each other too and, what's more, even their own poop! Sweet.

HARDY BOYS AND HARDY GIRLS

In the film *Wall-E*, the last survivors on earth are a robot (Wall-E) and his best friend—a cockroach. These insects are great survivors, not only because they give birth to so many, but also because they have some crazy abilities. For instance:

- Some cockroaches can live without food for a month!
- Others can go without air for forty-five minutes!
- Yet others can recover after being immersed in water for half an hour!
- Some can survive hours of freezing temperatures!
- Roaches have more than twelve times the capacity to survive a nuclear bomb and its rays of humans!

WILD IN THE BACKYARD

Experiment done by scientists

Method: Catch a cockroach. Cut its head off.
Result: The head will be alive for a few hours—even the body. If you keep the head cold (say, in your fridge), it lives even longer.
Conclusion: There's a lot of time for the roach to make last wishes.

YES OR NO

1. People drank boiled cockroach tea to cure ills.
2. Cockroaches are made to fight as gladiators.
3. Roaches have not travelled to space.
4. Cockroaches like to be touched.

ANSWERS

1. yes

From ancient times, cockroaches have been used as medicine to cure ills and injuries. No, it was not only the ancient folks who did that. Today, cockroach farming is big in China. The cockroaches are dried and ground and used in medicines as well as cosmetics. Who knows, we may be putting dried cockroaches on our dry lips every day!

2. yes

People have developed cockroach fighting and racing as sports! Some kinds of cockroaches are kept as pets. The giant Madagascar hissing cockroach is a favourite. The American boxer (human, mind you) Freddie Roach was called La Cucaracha (The Cockroach). However, some kinds of cockroaches are bred to be fed to other pets who eat insects.

3. no

The cockroach Nadezhda (meaning hope) was sent by Russian scientists into space and it was the first land creature to give birth in space. Thirty-three little Nadezhdas in the spaceship! How cute.

4. yes

That is the reason they go and hide in thin cracks, where they are pressed from all sides. Now that's one massage-loving insect!

SUPERVILLAIN WASP

Who do you need to tackle a villain? No, not a hero. You need . . . a supervillain!

The mighty roaches fall prey to wasps. And how! The *Ampulex dementor* wasp is named after the soul-sucking Dementors that gave Harry Potter the creeps. The female wasp stings the cockroach in the head to create a zombie cockroach. She then takes her slave zombie to her burrow and lays her eggs right on the living roach. Once her larvae come out of the eggs, they start feeding on the live cockroach till they are ready to go face the world. Yikes! That's pretty gruesome, huh?

However, all insects are not villainous. In fact, many aren't, so relax! Some sprinkle colour in our lives as they play in our gardens. Even with our best fashion statements, we can't match their style.

FLUTTERING FAIRIES

Little winged fairies—yep, butterflies—flit and flutter in our gardens and backyards, dancing in the breeze, basking in the sun, closing and opening their wings sitting on a flower of our potted plant, having a cool, sweet drink of nectar. Decked in splashes of the most unbelievable shades, with the sunlight setting their colours on fire, they look good at all times—early in the morning and on lazy afternoons, in flashy springtime and in the blazing summer. We can't pull that off, however hard we try, especially early in the morning, can we?

Except Antarctica, where penguins roam around clad in their shiny black-and-white tuxedos, butterflies are found all over the world. They have been around for no less than forty million years! Fifteen to twenty thousand different kinds flitter around our planet. But these colourful celebrities, whom we gawk at every time they make an appearance, also get killed by us in large numbers. Yes, yes, global warming, development and all that, but in other ways too. When we take out our cars for a drive, especially in the spring, many butterflies crossing the roads get smashed by our windscreens. A passing butterfly, fluttering at its own sweet pace, can't dart away like a dog or a crow from a moving vehicle, you see.

MIGHTY MIGRATIONS

We might puff our chests out and congratulate ourselves on achieving great speeds with our speedy set of wheels, but some butterflies put us to shame as far as travel (and looks and flight and coolness and . . . oh dear!) is concerned. The star migrators are the orange-and-black monarch butterflies that migrate from the US and Canada to their winter holiday homes in Mexico and are back in the spring. They are day travellers and use the sun to find their way. The painted lady is another well-known traveller.

In India, there are great butterfly migrations during the monsoons. They stun and dazzle as their copper, bronze, black and snow-white, carroty-red, silver-grey, pansy-blue . . . bodies fly away into the clouds. They even use roads and mountains to find their way. Some are night travellers too, and use the moon and the stars to guide them.

Where did *you* travel last summer?

AAAND A FEW MORE QUESTIONS

1. What do butterflies feed on?
    a. nectar
    b. dung
    c. rotting flesh and fruit
    d. human sweat
    e. all of the above
2. What do butterflies love to bathe in?
    a. rain
    b. orange juice
    c. dewdrops
    d. mud
    e. coke

WILD IN THE BACKYARD

3. Butterflies taste through their
    a. proboscis (drinking straw)
    b. feet
    c. antennae
    d. eyes
    e. wings
4. The wings of butterflies are covered with
    a. fur
    b. petals
    c. scales
    d. hair
    e. all of the above
5. What is a butterfly's life cycle?
    a. egg, butterfly
    b. caterpillar, butterfly
    c. egg, caterpillar, butterfly
    d. egg, caterpillar, pupa, butterfly
    e. none of the above
6. How do butterflies defend themselves?
    a. showing off their bright colours
    b. carrying poison
    c. mimicry
    d. disguise
    e. all of the above

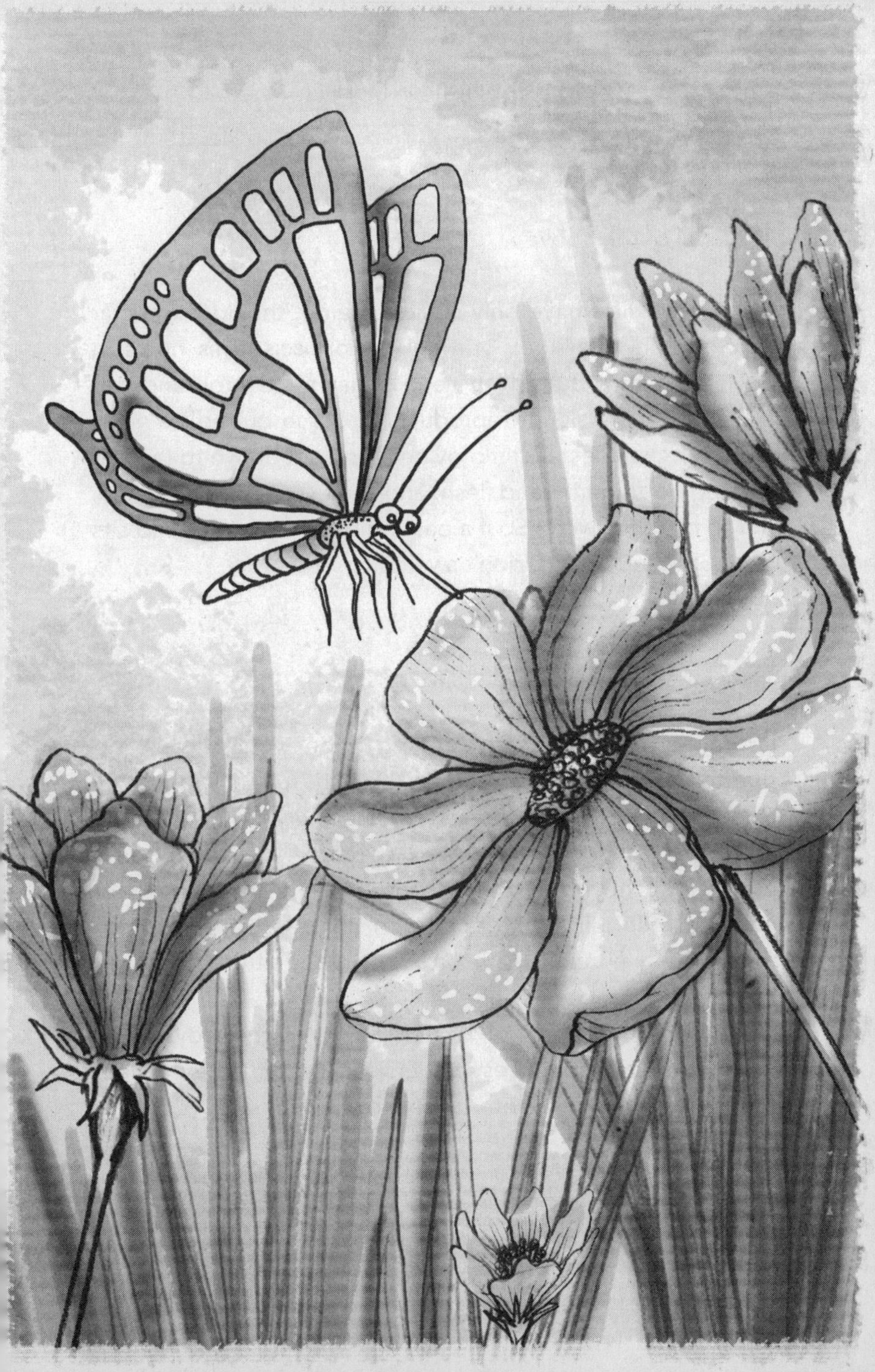

WILD IN THE BACKYARD

ANSWERS

1. e. all of the above

Adult butterflies have only liquids. Mainly, they drink nectar from flowers with their straw-like proboscis. This helps in pollination too. Butterflies need sugar for energy and salt and other minerals for reproduction. Some butterflies need more salt than nectar can provide. They get drawn to the salt in dung, rotting fruit and flesh, and can even land on people, drawn by their sweat! So if a passing butterfly comes and sits on your friend's hand, don't sweat it!

2. d. mud

This is the reason butterflies take mudbaths together. It's called mud-puddling. Ah . . . I'll bet you'd like to do that too! Butterflies don't just do that for fun, though. They also do it for the salt present in the mud. You can make mud pies at home for butterflies and even plant some plants that they love to visit. And your yard will be full of dancing little fairies! More tips on this can be taken from the Bombay Natural History Society. They often have their breakfasts with butterflies.

With some kinds of butterflies, only the boys have mudbaths, and some researchers reckon that they collect the salt for their sweethearts. Now that's sweet . . . or rather, salty!

3. b. feet

Butterflies taste with their feet. And their ability to taste is supposed to be 200 times greater than that of humans!

With their antennae of various shapes, sizes and colours, they sense the wind.

Their eyes are well-developed and many of them can see colours too. It would be a pity if they couldn't see their own brilliant colours, more dazzling than our disco lights.

4. c. scales

It is the tiny scales on their wings that give them their colours. These scales have melanin pigments (blacks and browns), resulting in the beautiful colours (red, blue, green, etc.) they wear.

Light, when it collides with matter, scatters. Why does the sky look blue? The blue light from the sun scatters more than the other colours of light when it bumps into the particles in our atmosphere. The scales of butterflies also scatter light. Depending on which colours they scatter most, they get their hues.

The powder left on your fingers after catching and releasing a butterfly is due to the scales they leave behind. Butterflies can't fly much once their wings are damaged.

5. d. egg, caterpillar, pupa, butterfly

Butterfly eggs are small and rounded, or oval, from which caterpillars emerge. The caterpillar first eats its own shell and then goes on to eat the leaf the eggs were stuck on. All it has on its mind is food, food and . . . well, food! The greedy caterpillar keeps on eating day in and day out. While most caterpillars are vegetarians and greatly mess up the plants they are born on, others stuff their bellies with insects. Some even go on to form great friendships with ants, who guard them, and they, in turn, supply the ants with yummy honeydew. The ever hungry caterpillar keeps growing and keeps shedding its skin to get a new one for its fatter body. When it is fully grown, it wanders until it finds a suitable leaf to hang on to. It then builds a pupa around itself and emerges from the pupa once winter ends. The fatso inside the pupa transforms into a slender, stunning butterfly. It steps out into the world, stretches and dries its wings, and then takes off.

This is called metamorphosis—a complete transformation. Like your dad transforms from really cool to hopping mad when he comes to know you've been playing games on his iPad during your study hours!

6. e. all of the above

Butterflies are beauties with brains! Caterpillars of some kinds of butterflies have developed ways to eat poisonous plants. The butterflies also carry this poison and they proudly display bright colours to warn predators that they are dangerous.

Some butterflies mimic the colours of their deadlier cousins to avoid hungry birds. An example is the female common mormon, who mimics the deadly red-bodied swallowtail.

There are some that look like leaves, freeze themselves to look like sticks or have colours that just blend in with the bark of a tree. Now these kinds of butterflies are generally of a green or earthy hue. 'What snooty oafs!' they'd probably be thinking of their brighter cousins.

Butterflies may live for a few days to a year, depending on what kind they are. But even if they live short lives, they know how to have a bash! They bask in the sun in the mornings (absorbing heat to fly during the day—they're cold blooded, after all!), chase other fluttering lads off their territories, show off their four fantastic wings day after day and flirt with the gulmohar, bougainvillea, nilofar, chameli, genda, champa and all the other flowers around them!

I bet you've had enough already of the genteel and the pretty. Now you're all set to look at some gory, blood-and-claws stuff, aren't you?

We have a host of different animals in our homes, backyards and cities in different seasons. But there's one that always rules the city sky. One steady look from it can give you butterflies in your stomach!

THE BLACK LORD OF THE SKIES

It swoops down from the dull blue sky, its dark wings flapping against the wind, strong talons outstretched and steely eyes glued to the kill. Before the unsuspecting lizard can draw up its will or even let out a howl, it is flying up and away into the sky, clutched in the long talons of the dark lord. It flies away remembering the best days of its life (the first meal of a crunchy grasshopper, the first sidelong glance from the spiky-skinned beauty . . .) before it is torn to shreds by the hooked beak looming large above it.

The dark lord of the city skies is the black kite, cruising and soaring on the air currents. While it may just appear to us as a dot in the sky, with its keen eyesight, it keeps a close watch on what's going on down where we live. It is a bird of prey, like hawks and eagles, and operates in day shifts unlike its cousin, the night worker, the owl.

CALL ME BLACK!

The black kite is a medium-sized raptor, that is, a bird of prey. Where did the word raptor come from? From the Latin word *rapere*, which means 'to take by force'.

Raptors are hunters. They feed on other animals. The black kite, until recently, was called the pariah kite, until some birders rubbed their hands, scratched their heads and decided to give it a better name. After thinking and thinking some more, they decided to call it . . . black! Howzat? I hope you're a little more imaginative than that!

Though it is dark brown with streaks, it looks almost black from a distance. The head is paler than the rest of the body.

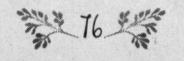

If you see it flying in the sky, you'll see it has a sort of a forked tail and angled wings. The girls and the boys look almost alike. Not like most other birds, where the boys are much better-looking than the girls. For instance, our jade-blue peacocks who dance all day long to impress the drab brown, uninterested ladies. Other than the boys and girls looking alike, there are a few other interesting facts about these city hunters.

FIVE DARK FACTS ABOUT BLACK

1. There are about six million black kites in the world!
   These serious-looking birds with pointed beaks mean business. They are supposed to be the world's most common birds of prey. In India, this raptor is found widely. We can often see them circling our cities and towns, looking down at us from the skies above. They thrive on living close to humans. Since we in India have a lot of humans milling about, the kites are in abundance too! According to a survey done in 1967, there were fifteen pairs of kites in 1 sq. km in Delhi! That is 2200 pairs in 150 sq. km! If we do that survey today, there might be many more, due to our increased numbers. Did I say six million black kites found all over the world? Bah, we are twenty-one million already in the city of Mumbai alone . . . Guess only rats and roaches can beat us in numbers. We're not in fine company, if I may say so.
2. Black kites not only hunt, they feed on the dead too.
   A shrill whistle followed by whining, and you know there is a black kite in the area. They glide and soar in the hot

air high up without using much energy. From there, they gaze down, searching for food. The kites in our cities aren't very fussy and are good with garbage, carrion, small birds, bats, rats and insects. They are both hunters and scavengers. You can see them gliding in groups high up in the sky and changing direction with ease. Sometimes, they fly low and gather around buildings. It's possible there's some dead animal or garbage dumped there, smelling worse than your morning breath! These kites can even snatch away nests of birds like bayas to feed on their eggs. They prefer their eggs raw, not scrambled or sunny side up!

In Udaipur, a city in Rajasthan, an interesting observation was made by Dr Raza Tehsin, the naturalist. He saw that these kites sit facing the setting sun when they go to roost. And in the mornings, they sit facing the rising sun. Guess they do like sunny side up, after all!

3. Where there's fire, there's . . . a kite?

   Some native people of Australia believed that kites spread fire by dropping burning twigs around. Now now, that's not true. They do get drawn to smoke and fire (they don't cause it, though) but to catch some smoked prey trying to escape—it's going to roast anyway!

4. They will attack you if you go too near their nest.

   The ma and pa kites taking care of their baby kites can be pretty nasty towards anyone who tries to tinker with their nests, or even come close to them. And they remember if you've been anywhere close before! If you try to do it a second time, they might just dive down and gouge out

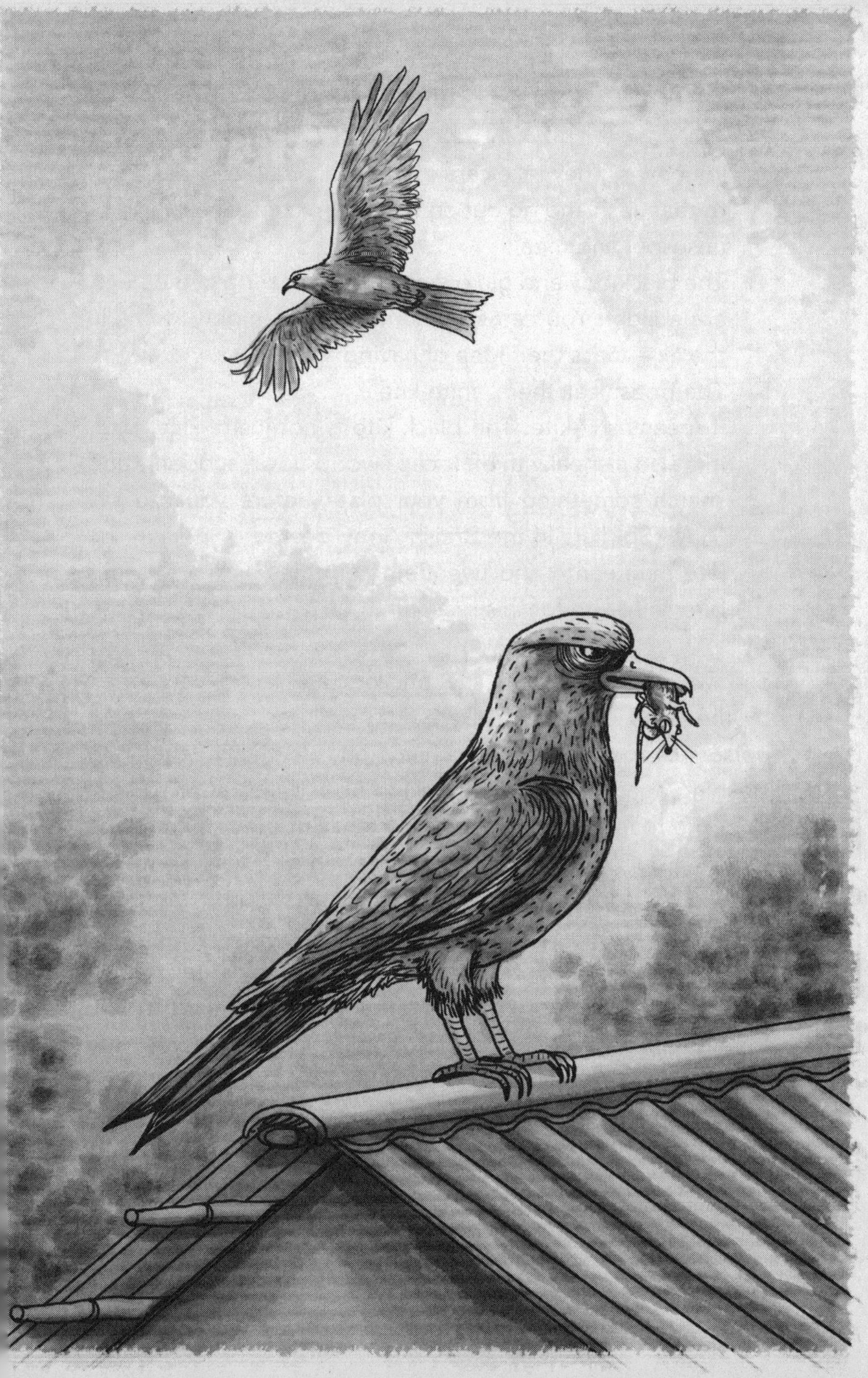

your eyes! They take care of their chicks till they are ready to tear flesh and go out on their own to find their dead or unsuspecting meal.

The black boy and girl out on a date, soaring in the skies, are a sight! You can see them perform mighty stunts in the air—that's their idea of having a great time.

5. The British call them 'shite-kite'.

It means shit-kite. The black kite is not just a killer bird, it is also a sneaky thief. It can swoop down suddenly and snatch something from your plate before you can say 'Hey!' Soldiers in the British Army posted in India in the late nineteenth and twentieth centuries nicknamed this bird shite-kite for this reason.

The whistle-voiced, city-savvy killers are killed very often by the ways of humans. By eating polluted food or dead, poisoned rodents, by perching on electricity wires, by crashing against cars when picking up a dead rat or squirrel from the road and so on and so forth. But they still manage to live in our cities with us. The Egyptian goddess Isis is said to take the form of a kite when she has to bring the dead back to life.

Though black kites might look scary with their mobs, which even the glossy crows fear, you have nothing to fear from them. The ones that you should be wary of are the blokes that bare their teeth at you if you act smart, or snatch away your ice cream even if you're *not* acting smart! It's no wonder then that they're our cousins and are so much like us.

MONKEY
LORE

Jumping from wall to wall or branch to branch, the black-faced monkeys move about towns and villages, confident in their monkey business in the homes of their cousins—human beings. The grey or Hanuman langurs believe they belong in the cities as much as in the jungles. They sit on trees or rooftops, picking out each other's dead skin and lice and putting them in their mouths to munch on—a crisp, in-between-meals snack. Or their troupes bounce from electricity poles to car tops to boundary walls. And what do we do? We look at them in awe or yelp and scat! If you observe closely, you'll see a glint of mischief in their eyes. They seem to know they are better than their tailless cousins.

BURNT-FACE HANUMAN

The Story Behind the Monkey's Name

The Ramayana says that when Hanuman went to save Sita from Lanka and purposely set the place on fire, he burnt his hands and his face. And lo! The Hanuman langur has a face, ears and hands as black as coal! In India, they say the langur is holy and to kill it is a sin. After all, how would Rama have crossed the sea to Lanka without the monkeys' help? The army of monkeys built him a safe and sturdy bridge over the sea.

This is all very nice. But it doesn't stop people from eating monkeys. And that's not all. Some people even use monkey teeth and paws to make charms that dangle from their wrists and necks! Sadly, humans do more monkey business than monkeys themselves.

AREFA TEHSIN

LANKY LANGURS

Hanuman langurs are found throughout South Asia:

- near seas
- in deserts
- in dry jungles
- in rainforests
- and even in the Himalayas (as high up as 13,000 ft!)

These langurs are quite at home in towns as well as in villages. You won't find them in your backyard or garden every day, but they might visit you once in a while. Or you might chance upon them in someone else's backyard or at a picnic spot or a temple, eyeing everyone's food. A bold one may even step down and snatch away someone's ice cream!

They get most of their water from the food they eat, so they actually drink water only sometimes. At night, they sleep on high branches, poles or towers. In the jungles, when they eat fruits, they make a crazy mess and drop a lot of it on the ground. Their friends—the birds and deer—clear it off by chomping on the crunchy bits.

TERRIFIC TAILS

There are seven kinds of Hanuman langurs. They are lanky and swift, with tails longer than their bodies. The north Indian ones have their tails pointing forwards. The south Indian ones have their tails pointing backwards in an inverted U or S shape.

The tail helps them balance as they leap, walk on branches, hop on two legs or walk coolly on four. The young ones somersault or tumble with their friends, jump down in the water to have a splashing time, swing on branches, play-tussle with or tease each other and run away. Monkeys sure know how to have fun! You should send your pa and ma to go and learn from the monkey elders, who let their kids have fun all the time!

DON'T BABY ME!

The pale-skinned, dark-haired baby monkeys, who cling to their mothers for a free ride everywhere, lie low only till the time they grow up enough to move around. Then they can be cranky, cry at the top of their voices and throw a fit, just like human babies do. Mamas don't pay them much attention once they know what their brats are up to.

NAUGHTY MONKEYS

The little baby monkeys, with wrinkled faces that look upon the world with wide-eyed wonder, become impish and playful boys and girls with time. Given the way we humans are, there's no knowing if they'll grow up to be moody, quiet, caring, clever, bossy, hot-tempered, lazy, loud show offs, the usual morons or all of these.

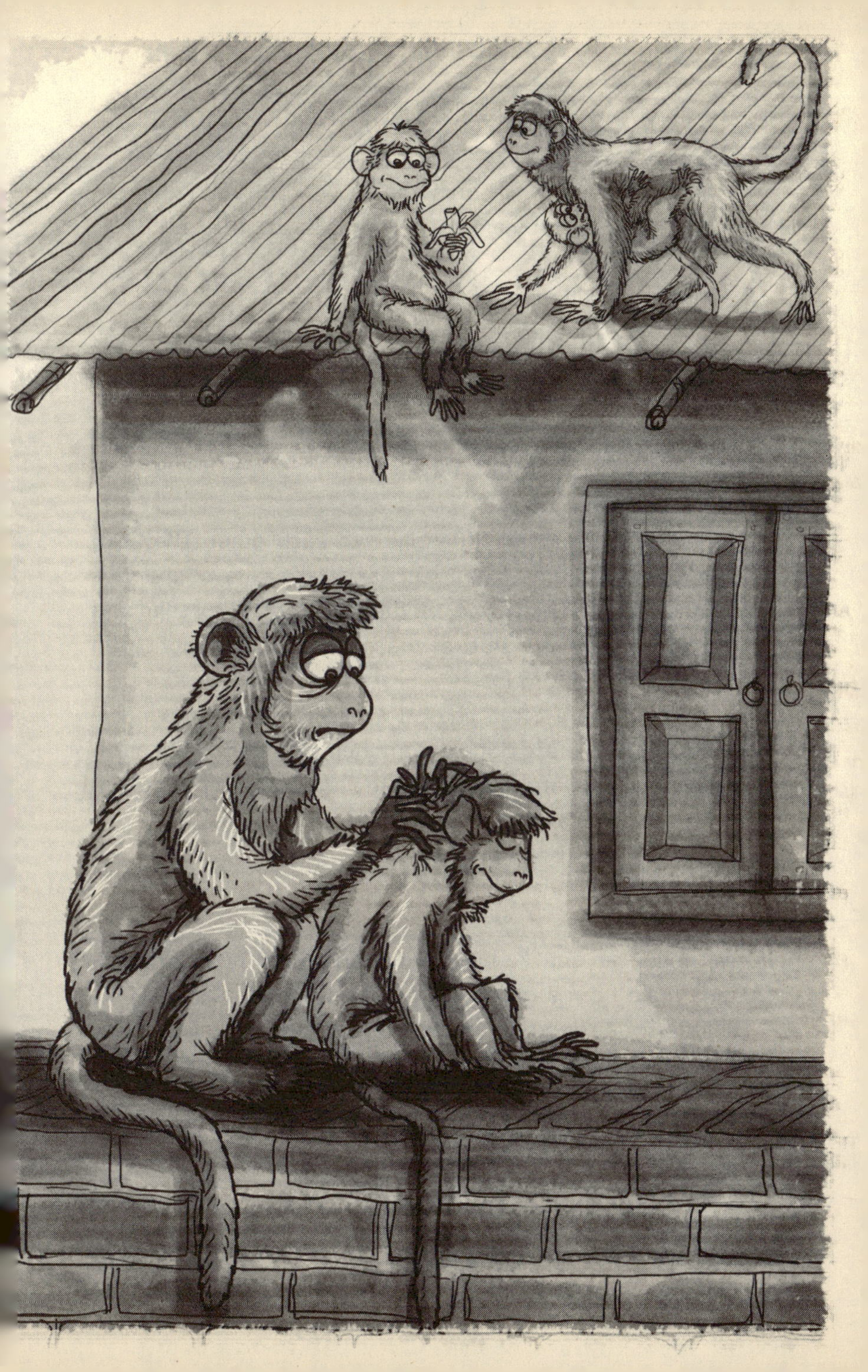

In the case of the langurs, the grown-ups live in different kinds of group combinations:

- one gent with a lot of ladies and kids
- all boys together, sneering at the all-gals' groups, that is, of course, till they find their sweethearts
- both gents and ladies in a mixed group

GROOVY GANG WARS

The ladies are generally friendly with each other. They eat, travel, groom themselves, sleep and take care of the kids together. It's the gents who are the rowdy lot. They snarl and fight to become the stud of the group. Or they fight with males from other groups.

The boys are often chased away from the group at a young age and these drifters form their own all-boys' groups. These boys then attack and fight the leaders of other groups and chase them away to become the new leaders.

Baby Killers

Yes, gents can act like hoodlums when they chase away the alpha male from a group to become the new bosses—they kill little squeaking babies who are not their own. *Some* way to gain the ladies' attention!

AREFA TEHSIN

MONKEY TALK

Ah . . . yes, monkeys talk all the time. Not as much as we do, though.

Harsh warning calls: Although the Hanuman langurs just eat leaves, fruits, pods and other vegetable matter, they make for yummy meals for tigers, jackals, dholes (wild dogs), wolves and even pythons! And they are a special favourite of leopards—a leopard may even climb a tree to catch a monkey. *(Leopard: Burrrp! What a marvellous monkey meal!)* The monkeys go nuts if they see a leopard in the area. They start to jump from branch to branch or fart and poop in fear. Let's hope you're never caught standing under such a tree!

Rumblings: They softly rumble, either when the gent approaches the lady, muttering sweet nothings, or when the ladies sit hunch-backed, picking lice and gossiping or during other such laid-back times.

Honks, grunts, loud calls, screams and pant-barks: This happens when different groups come across each other. The top males bare their teeth ferociously and make loud whooping sounds, trying to scare away other males. They can be big and scary. The heaviest recorded langur was a Nepal grey langur that weighed 26.5 kg!

Cough-barks and hiccups: They cough-bark when the group is moving from one place to another. Or hiccup when they come across another group.

Well, coming across the Kashmir grey langurs would probably not happen all that often. There are only around 250 of them left in the world. Of the seven kinds of langurs, this one is the rarest. So is the black-footed grey langur. Seems this one burnt its foot, too, in Lanka!

THICK FRIENDS

Langurs are good friends with cheetals in the wild. A cheetal is a deer that wears a stylish spotted coat. Langurs pluck fruits and throw them on the ground for the cheetals. Since these monkeys can see long distances from their trees, they warn the cheetals if there is a leopard or any other hunter nearby. What do the cheetals do for them? Maybe nod and say a warm thank you! Some people have even observed monkeys riding on the back of a cheetal to cross a river! Now, if that isn't friendship, what is?

NEEM HAKEEM

The langurs change their diets according to the time of the year and the kind of place they're living in. Sometimes, they eat fruits and flowers. At others, ripe leaves, and at yet other times, the barks of trees when nothing else is available.

Langurs also know what to eat to treat their illnesses. And they don't shirk from eating healthy!

A Hanuman langur once took shelter on a neem tree in the garden of Dr Raza H. Tehsin, a jungle wanderer and wildlifer. The monkey was hurt, lonely and sad—he had probably been in a fight with a dog. Dr Raza kept some roti and water for him below the tree and he came down and had some water but didn't touch the roti. For five days, he kept chewing only neem leaves, not touching the fresh, tempting roti even once. After five days he walked away from the tree, all springy and almost healed.

DOGGONE DOGS!

Hanuman langurs and dogs are not exactly on very friendly terms. They bark at each other, bare their teeth and make quite a display. Sometimes, a bold langur will even come down and slap a dog and quickly climb back up the tree! There, it smugly munches on the leaves as the frustrated dog barks its head off.

These dog-and-monkey fights can be seen in towns where monkey gangs roam. The arid city of Jodhpur in Rajasthan is as famous for its sweets as it is for its gangs of Hanuman langurs. They hang around homes and shops and don't wait to be handed out goodies—they just walk in and snatch them anyway! With throngs of people giving these holy monkeys food in temples and gardens, they have become fearless. They steal food, raid crops and even bite if you try to act funny with them. They don't like monkey business from others!

If You Pay Peanuts, You Get Monkeys

In the 2010 Commonwealth Games hosted in Delhi, city-bred Hanuman langurs were trained to patrol the stadiums and nearby living areas to chase out other wild animals like dogs, wild monkeys and snakes!

We may dissolve into giggles looking at monkeys behaving funnily, but they sure can make even our parliament dance if they so wish! In India, there are around 3,00,000 Hanuman langurs. Just one or two are enough to scare us out of our wits! The officers in Delhi trained forty youths to dress and act like monkeys to shoo them away from the VVIP areas. What a fun job! Unless, of course, a monkey decides to have a bite-fight with you. Now, that won't be pretty!

By the way, monkeys are not the only ones that bite. Got a scratch in your head? Lousy, isn't it?

LOUSY LICE

While we go around looking for the wild in our backyards and sinks and drains, there may be a host of them living on our heads! The louse, with six closely placed legs ending in sharp hooks, and a fat transparent belly, goes about its evening walk camouflaged in our hair to digest the blood it fed on earlier. Well, lice, really, in the plural. Since it doesn't live alone but by the dozen. Lice suck your blood as you would suck a lollypop!

SCRATCH SCRATCH, WHO IS IT?

There are no less than 3000 kinds of lice found in the world! They are wingless insects that live on birds and mammals. They are divided into two kinds:

- chewing lice
- sucking lice

Chewing lice are scavengers and crunch on dead skin and other waste on the body. Sucking lice feed on blood. Different animals have different lice on them. For some unfortunate creatures, different kinds of lice are found on different parts of their bodies! You can scratch yourself bloody but not get rid of them.

FIVE LOUSY FACTS

1. Some animals can have up to fifteen different kinds of lice on them! But generally, mammals have about one

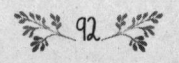

to three kinds of lice. And birds have about two to six kinds.
2. They love you to death! If you remove a louse from the animal or bird it lives on, after a while, the louse will die.
3. Their colour changes when they feed on blood. Generally, they are pale brown or dark grey. But when they feed on blood, their colour darkens many shades.
4. There are more females than males and their young are like miniature adults. Unlike butterflies and some other insects that have a pupa stage, lice have miniature, adult-like little ones. They shed their skins three times—which is called moulting—before they reach the size of a grown-up.
5. Dead lice eggs are yellow and living ones are pale white. The mama head lice in humans have special saliva to stick their eggs to our hair. And these eggs, also called nits, are *really* difficult to remove! The lice living on birds, however, don't bother gluing their eggs to the bird. They simply lay them in areas which the poor bird can't reach with its beak or claws, like the insides of its feathers.

Humans have three different kinds of lice on them:

- head lice
- body lice
- pubic lice

They are all sucking lice.

In World War I, a soldier, on an average, had twenty lice on his body. The record holder is a soldier who had more than 10,000 lice and more than 10,000 nits!

> *Did you know . . .*
>
> Lice have helped researchers and scientists make new discoveries about human evolution!

CHIMPS AND US

Scientists have been scratching their heads to figure out our relation with apes—here's where the lice come in. Our relation with lice and apes goes back millions of years in history, before we parted from the chimpanzees. Lice found on human heads and bodies and those found in chimpanzees have a common ancestor. Our pubic lice share the same ancestor as the lice found on gorillas. We descended from the apes. These bloodsuckers are proof of that.

The popular theory among anthropologists—those who study where human beings came from—is the out-of-Africa theory (OOA). And according to that, we evolved from apes into modern humans in Africa and then moved out to other continents. The greater variety of human lice found in Africa suggests that there were humans there before any other place on earth. Fancy that—we might all have been Africans!

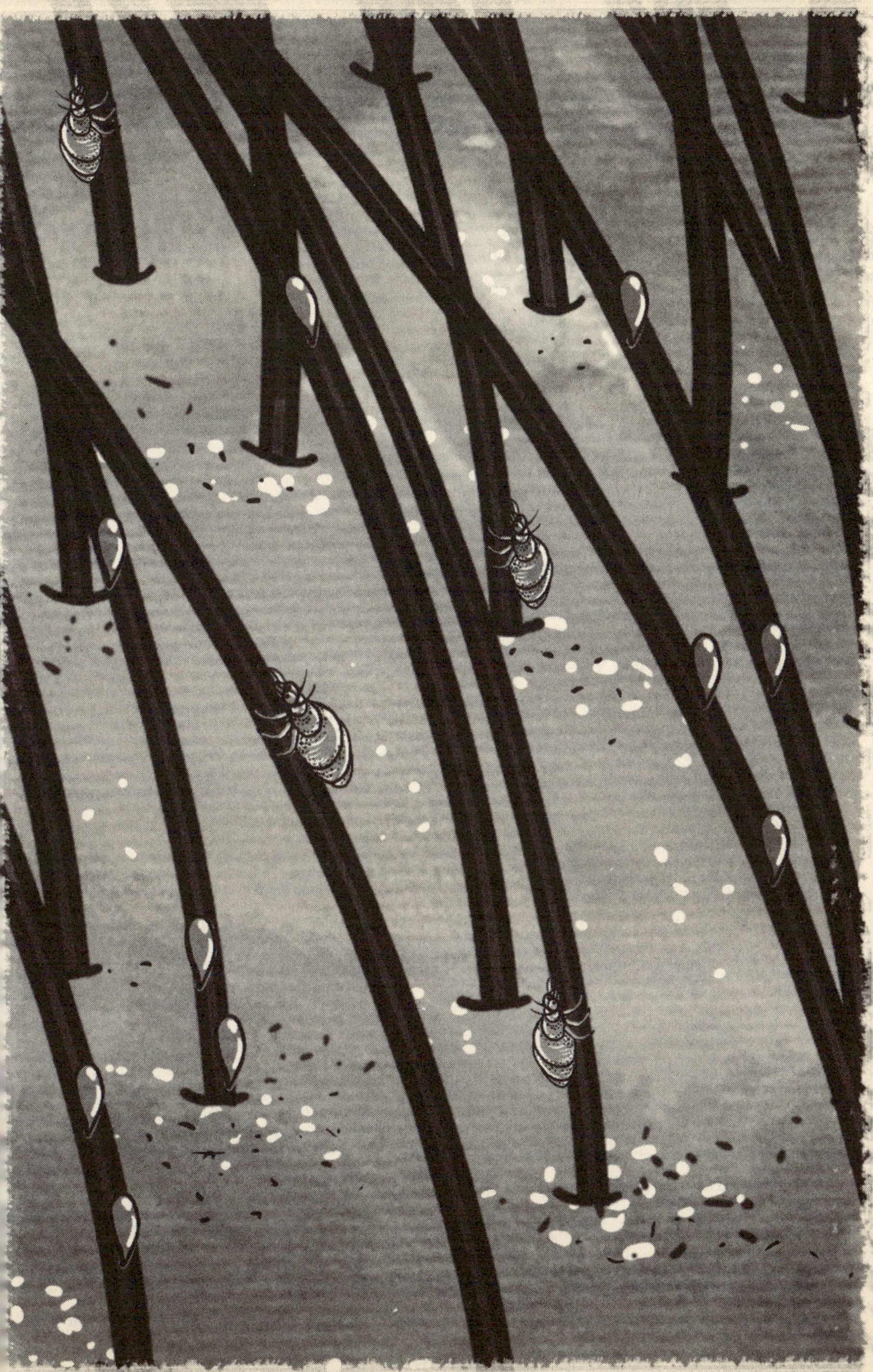

WILD IN THE BACKYARD

TRUE OR FALSE

1. Lice are found in all mammals.
2. The poop of head lice is red.
3. Head lice spread diseases.
4. Head lice like shadows and dark-coloured objects.
5. Head lice can jump from head to head.
6. Head lice can't attend school.
7. Shaving the head can control lice infestation.

ANSWERS

1. false

Although lice are found in all kinds of birds, there are a few mammals that don't have lice. Like bats, whales and dolphins.

2. true

They feed on blood four to five times a day by biting into the skin. Their special saliva does not let the blood clot for some time, till their bellies are full. Their poop is dark red!

3. false

Head lice do not spread diseases. But body lice do. They can spread typhus, trench fever and relapsing fever. These tiny tots, the size of sesame seeds, can leave you drooling in your beds.

4. true

They do not like the light. That is why they prefer to hang around the nape of the neck or the area behind the ear. They usually lay their eggs there.

5. false

Head lice do not jump from one head to another with a heart-stopping thud! Their legs are too weak to jump. And they do not have angel wings. They just crawl using their claw-like legs from one head to the other when heads meet.

Lice can't swim either. That is why some people in India pick lice out of their hair and put them in a bowl full of water.

6. true

Well, in some countries at least. Head lice are most common in children aged three to twelve. Since lice move from head to head, countries like the US and Canada have come up with a 'no-nit policy'. Children who have lice in their hair can't attend school till they are completely lice and nit free.

7. true

We have struggled since the age of cavemen to get rid of the lice on our heads. Dried lice have been found on the heads of mummies as well! We've been trying and trying over centuries to find easy ways to remove lice. These treatments include lotions and shampoos, natural remedies (tea tree oil, salt and vinegar, neem oil, etc.), lice combs and even hot air! Iodine is an antiseptic used on wounds, and some people paint iodine on the affected areas to get rid of lice.

If you've had lice at any point of time, you might recall that itch. You might also remember pulling one from your hair and crunching it to a pulp between your nails. Ah, that wonderful feeling! But there are some creatures you can't imagine holding in your hand or crunching between your fingers. Like those creeps with all the legs!

THE HUNDRED LEGGER

One of the oldest animals on earth (It has been around for 430 million years!)—a venomous predator—rises as night falls in your cosy, peaceful home. What do you expect next? Centipedes—meaning, a hundred legs—are not easy to spot in Indian homes or gardens. But when you come across one, you might just cry, fart or choke in horror as if you had swallowed a frog or seen your mark sheet!

Centipedes—there are 8000 kinds, by the way—are not insects as they have more than six feet. *Way* more! They roam around in the outdoors, sometimes in your gardens or garages, turning your tummies to water. But it is when they step indoors, into your bedrooms and sinks, that you feel truly trapped. They are found in deserts and forests and homes and gardens and even beyond the Arctic Circle! So there really is no escape.

They have a pair of venomous claws near their flat or rounded mouths. And they are all carnivorous. They use their antennae—the two feelers on the top of their heads—to locate yummy dinner. And once they find a crispy spider or crunchy beetle, they use their venomous claws to kill it. Their bodies are divided into segments and each segment has a pair of legs. The numbers of legs vary in different kinds of centipedes. They can be drab or brightly coloured—like the Indian tiger centipede that has bright orange stripes. It walks through the grass like a flickering flame and its bite definitely feels like one.

AREFA TEHSIN

A HUNDRED QUESTIONS (UM ... ACTUALLY ONE-TWENTIETH OF THAT)

1. How many legs do centipedes not have?
   a. 100
   b. 96
   c. 30
   d. 34
   e. 42
2. What do centipedes like most?
   a. a midnight snack
   b. a cool, moist chill-out place
   c. a relaxed evening walk
   d. a short snooze in the daytime
   e. a scratch on the back
3. Which of the following statements is true?
   a. Mama centipedes take care of the young.
   b. Mama centipedes don't take care of the young.
   c. Mama centipedes eat their own eggs if upset.
   d. Baby centipedes eat their mamas.
   e. all of the above
4. What problems can a centipede bite cause in humans?
   a. weakness
   b. allergy
   c. chills and fever
   d. swelling
   e. any or all of the above

WILD IN THE BACKYARD

5. Which of the given statements is true?
    a. Some centipedes don't have eyes.
    b. A few centipedes grow legs with age.
    c. Spiders prey on centipedes and centipedes prey on spiders.
    d. all of the above
    e. none of the above

ANSWERS

1. a. 100

Yes. Centipedes *don't* have 100 legs! Centipedes can have 30 to more than 300 legs, but not 100. Why on earth? It's because they only have odd numbers of pairs—say, 49 or 51 pairs, which makes 98 or 102 legs (but never 100).

Each pair of legs is a little longer than the one in the front. This way, they do not fumble and roll over when they have to run quickly. At times, the last pair can be almost double the length of the first!

2. b. a cool, moist chill-out place

Although most centipedes like coming out at night to enjoy a midnight snack, what they like most is a wet or moist place to hang out. Wherever they live, in deserts or forests, they always look for a moist place to lounge about. They do not have a waxy coating on their cuticles (cuticle is insect skin, whether cute or not!) like insects do and so tend to lose water

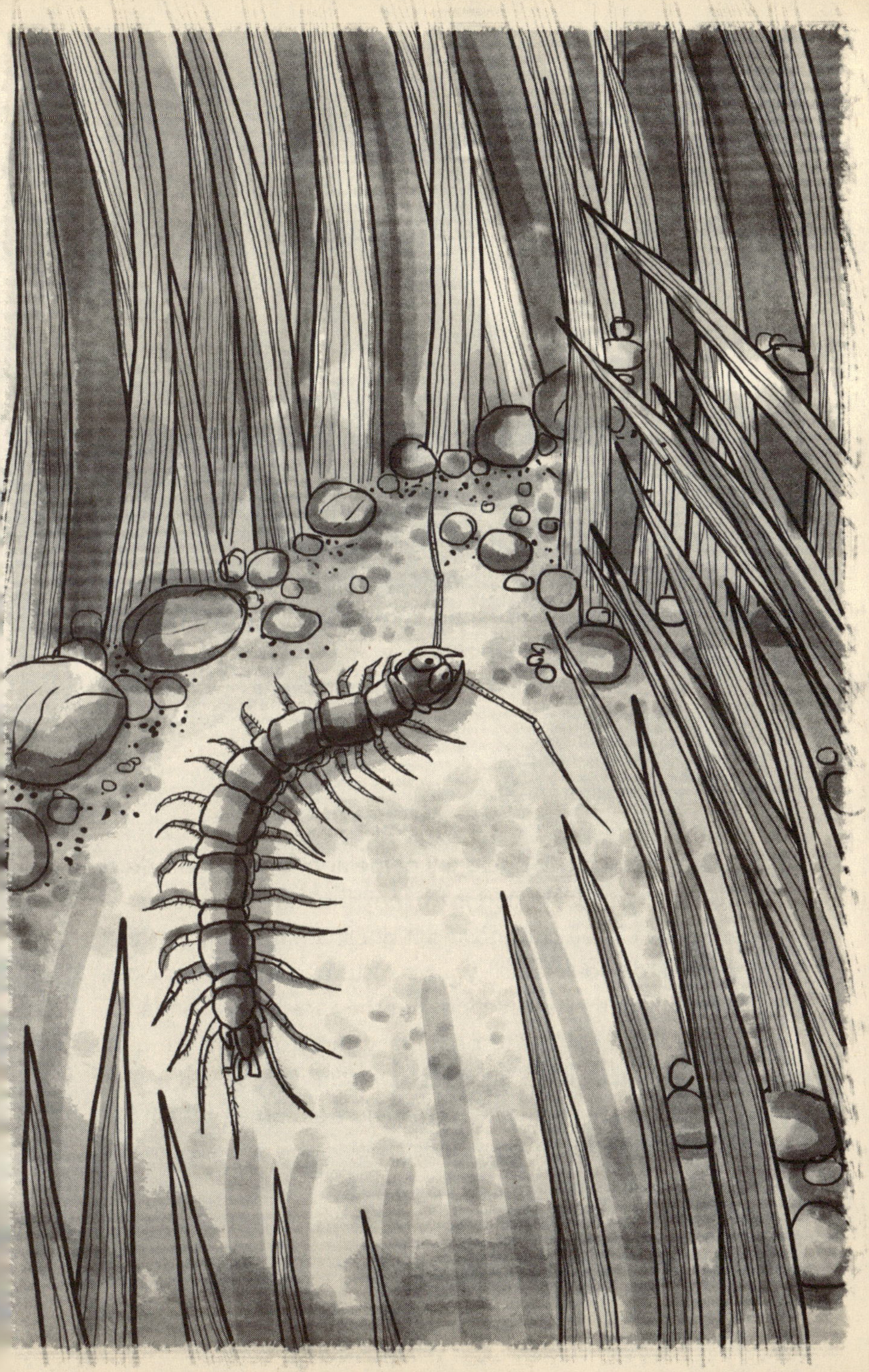

from their bodies quickly. So a nice litter of leaves, a cosy space under the soil, large stones or a pile of sticks is their ideal chill-out place.

3. e. all of the above

Yes. All of the above. How can that be true? It can be, if there are thousands of different kinds of centipedes who have their own lifestyles. Some mama centipedes take care of their eggs. Some take care of their young ones too. A few mamas can eat their own eggs if they think they're in danger. What's more, some centipede babies feast on the first available fresh meal once they're out of their egg—their own mamas!
Baby: Mama, I'm hungry . . .
Mama: Oh no, my dear! I am not served with tomato ketchup!

4. e. any or all of the above

Yes, yes. It can cause one or all of the above. But don't worry, it won't kill you. Centipedes do look frightful, being some of the leggiest of all critters, and it doesn't help a bit that they rush towards your feet if you've disturbed a table or closet behind which they lay resting. But they are not as dangerous as we make them out to be. In fact, most of them are quite harmless as they can't puncture our skin.

In Hindi, they are called *kankhajura* as some of them find our ears (*kaan*) to be cosy beds. They come and lie down in a semicircle, their legs curled around our ear's edge. Such a nice way to sleep, no?

5. d. all of the above

Oh, yes. All of these are correct. Centipedes don't have good eyesight. Some don't have eyes at all!

Either the centipedes are born with all their legs, or they grow them with age—one pair at a time! Like the American house centipede. It is born with four pairs of legs and as it grows, it moults (sheds its skin). After each round of moulting, it grows a new pair of legs—five, seven, nine . . . till it reaches fifteen! With most centipedes, the gents have fewer legs than the ladies; maybe to let the ladies pass by first.

Male centipede: Ma'am, I insist. After you . . .

Yes, spiders and centipedes prey on one another. It depends on who's the bigger or stronger of the two. Centipedes don't exactly have a very refined palate; they eat anything they can take down. The smaller centipedes eat insects for the most part. The bigger ones, like the Amazonian giant centipede (around 30 cm long, the largest in the world!), hunt bats, mice, frogs, spiders and even birds, before they can take off in flight! Now that's groovy.

But what goes around comes around. Centipedes eat some, and then get eaten some—as crunchy lunches and scrumptious dinners—by snakes, beetles, mice and mongooses.

WILD IN THE BACKYARD

They do try defending themselves—they bite, use their claws or even try running away as fast as their numerous legs can carry them. They don't always get away, though.

But so what if they're fast runners? Hah, big deal! If you had a hundred legs, you too would run wild! But what about a thousand-legged, slow animal? Right there in your own backyard that too!

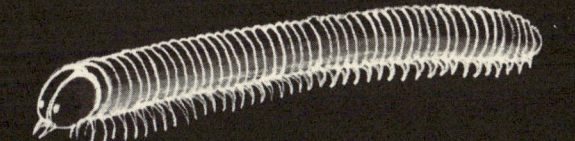

THE
THOUSAND
LEGGER

What's faster than a hundred legger? A thousand legger? You'd think, wouldn't you? But no. Millipedes—meaning, a thousand legs—move their many legs slowly, like endless little waves. They move their long, tube-shaped bodies neatly, checking out the world with their antennae, which are as slow-moving as they are. Some millipedes are friends with mosses and ants, at war with birds and badgers and have nothing to do with their distant cousins—centipedes—though they might both look quite similar to us. Well, that's not saying much, since we probably look the same to them.

Student millipede: Is that human Indian? Chinese? Geez . . . I hate biology!

Just as there is no centipede with 100 legs, there is no millipede with 1000. Some guy from ages past probably just looked at a millipede, too afraid or too lazy to count its legs, and said, 'This little fellow has 1000 legs!' They actually have much fewer than that. The record holder for the most number of legs is the giant African millipede with 750 legs. It is believed to be the creature with the most legs on earth!

WE'RE PEDES, ALL RIGHT, BUT WE'RE DIFFERENT

Both the centipede and millipede can make you weep or scream or swoon—imagine you're brushing your teeth at night (because your mum ordered you to) and one comes happily creeping out of the wash basin! They both have bodies divided into segments and are among the oldest land animals on earth. Both of them can hardly see and some of them are completely blind. They both have a pair of antennae and a lot of legs. And they both prefer moist places to live in as they do not have a waxy coating on their skin to preserve water in their bodies. Yet, they are different. Let's see how.

	Centipede	Millipede
1	One pair of legs per segment	Two pairs of legs per segment
2	Meat eaters	Mostly eat vegetables and decaying matter
3	Venomous	Non-venomous
4	Move fast	Move slowly

I'M ON A DIET OF THE DEAD AND DECAYING

That's what millipedes love to munch on—decaying leaves, animal poop and other such yummies mixed with a dash of soil. Some millipedes eat fresh leaves and gorge on our crops. Others eat fungi and tree bark or drink plant juices. There are only a few who are carnivorous and eat insects as well as their distant cousin, the centipede.

Together they can eat all the leaf litter of an area. Their poop is in the form of smooth, round pellets which, in turn, are eaten by bacteria and other tiny creatures, making it rot and recycling the soil. Phew . . . what would we do without millipedes to recycle all the litter and poop lying around?

WILD IN THE BACKYARD

Let's see if you can match the correct answers to the questions below.

1. Where can some kinds of millipedes survive?
2. Where do some kinds of millipedes lay their eggs?
3. What do some kinds of millipedes use as defence?
4. Whom are some millipedes friends with?
5. What is the favourite food of the spotted snake millipede?

---

a. bristles b. sugar beet c. mosses d. underwater e. dried poop

---

CORRECT MATCHES

1. d. underwater

Some kinds of millipedes can live underwater for up to eleven months! Although, they'd rather live in forests, eating fallen leaves and rotting wood. They can even live in deserts and caves where they can find some moisture. In some moist forests, you can find a thousand millipedes in 1 sq m! Imagine that happening in your garden or porch! They generally live in flower beds and other such damp places in our gardens.

2. e. dried poop

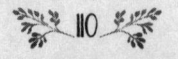

Yes, some kinds of millipedes line their nests with dried poop. Other kinds lay their eggs in moist soil or rotting leaves. There are around 12,000 kinds of millipedes found in the world and depending on the species, the ladies can lay 10–300 eggs at a time! As the babies grow into youngsters they keep shedding their skin and growing more legs each time, till they turn into adults. The common kinds have 34–400 legs. In the old, *old* days, there were millipedes 6–7 ft long! But now, the longest one is around 15 in.—to suit our size, not that of the dinosaurs.

3. a. bristles

Some kinds of millipedes have bristles. And it is wise to avoid them. If you brush past them, the bristles come off and lodge in your skin, making you itch till you cry! These bite-less, slow millipedes have other hip ways to defend themselves. Many of them can roll themselves into a ball when they sense danger—like a hungry cat or a pesky kid! A few millipedes let out a foul-smelling liquid, which can burn ants and cause itching or burns in larger animals. Some super-smart capuchin monkeys and lemurs upset these millipedes and then rub the awful-smelling liquid on their skins to repel mosquitoes!

4. c. mosses

There is a kind of millipede—the *P. bryophorus*—that carries various kinds (up to ten) of mosses on its back. The mosses hide the millipede from predators and they, in turn, get a free ride on its back!

5. b. sugar beet

The spotted snake millipede is considered a pest to farming as it has a weakness for sugar beet. Can't blame the chap for having a sweet tooth, now! Apart from a few who feed on crops, millipedes are not harmful to humans. In fact, some large ones are even kept as pets.

- In some Nigerian cultures, millipedes are crushed and used to treat fever and fits in children.
- In Zambia, millipede pulp is used to treat wounds.
- The Bobo people of western Africa eat boiled and dried millipedes with tomato sauce.
- Some Himalayan tribes smoke dried millipedes to treat piles.

If a millipede comes across a human, it just finds another route and crawls on. But we either get scared, scream and crush them to death, or we savour them—boiled or dried—with tomato sauce. And we have the nerve to call *them* pests!

RAIN, RAIN, COME AGAIN!

Rains are crazy, wild times for many creatures. Insects come out to live their lives as if there is no tomorrow. Toads create a racket with their calls and frogs jump out of the mud with plops. Mosquitoes swarm above our heads in a wild dance and sway in rhythm as we wave our hands about! Red and black ants come out in armies, invading homes. Termites

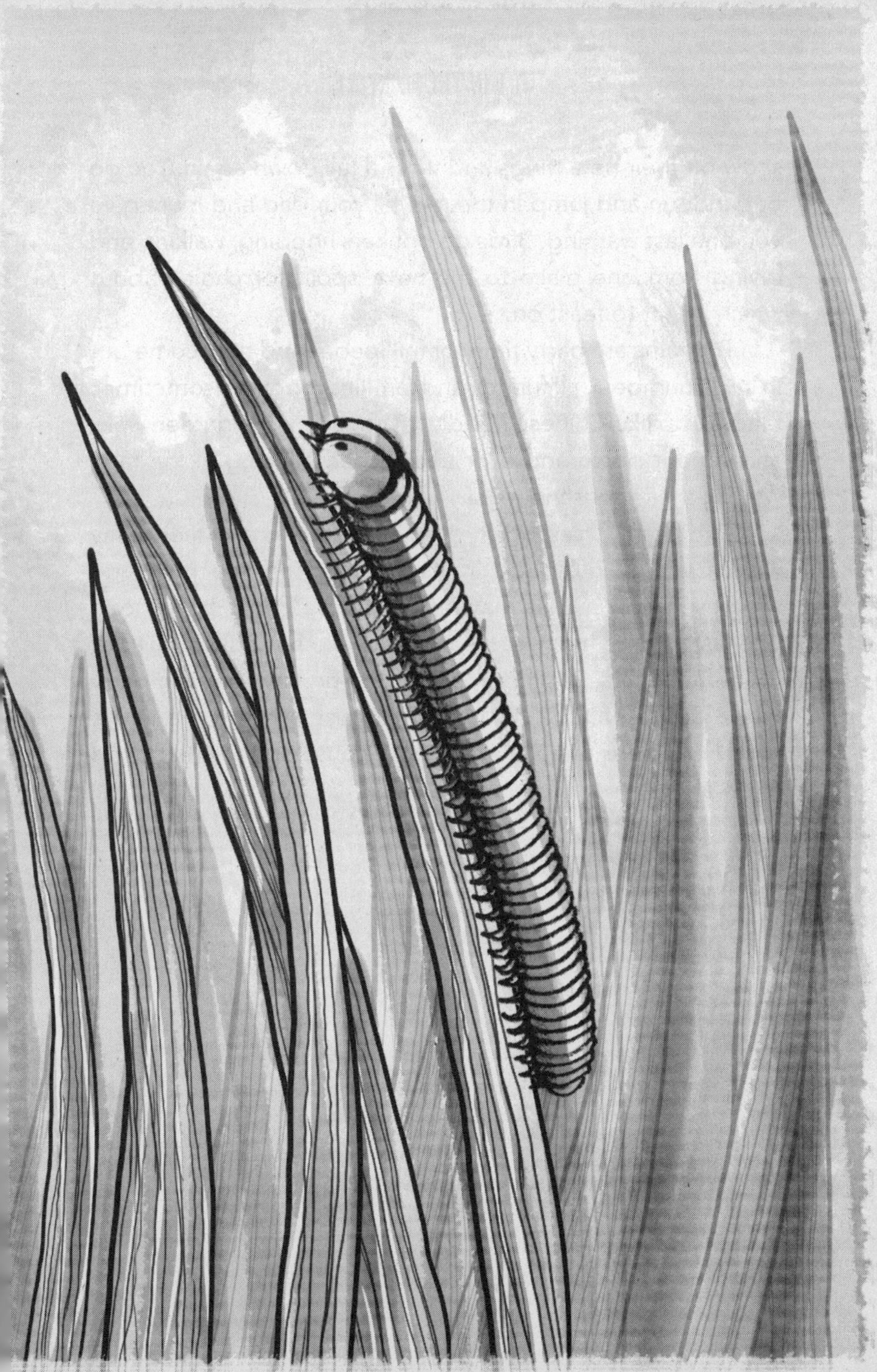

show off their new wings and fly and fall down again. You go out and run and jump in the rain till your dad and mum give you one last warning. Birds go bonkers hopping, walking and diving from one place to the next, spoilt for choice about which insect to feast on.

The rains are party time for millipedes and they come out in large numbers, all friends and families together, sometimes tangled up like Chinese noodles. They sit on the garden walls and on our porch and over each other, dancing in the rain, waving their thousand legs!

And there dives down a house sparrow and flies away with a wiggly millipede in its mouth. And the millipede wiggles, thinking that maybe, *maybe* he could have gone one last time to his sweetheart and make her go weak in her thousand knees. But if he was so bent on having a rain party in the open, without the fear of a house sparrow, he was a fool! For where there is a house, a house sparrow is bound to be about.

THE HYPER LITTLE BIRDIES

With a squiggling, protein-rich millipede in its beak, the house sparrow flies to its nest and stuffs it down the throat of its ever-hungry chicks. And the featherless, shivering little chicks in the nest shout their heads off, wanting more. The tired papa or mama flies off again, looking for a dreamy earthworm or an insect that's busy trying to flap and show off its wings.

The sparrow couple has a variety to choose from, especially in the rains, to feed the ever-hungry chicks a dozen times a day! There are a host of insects and other critters out and about, flying or crawling around during the day and dancing madly around the lights at night. But there are other hunters up and about on trees, bushes, flower beds, boundary walls, hedges, grasses and porches, eyeing the same feast. The masked mynahs go around with their angry faces, looking like Batman about to strike down the Joker. The garden lizards jump, catch insects mid-air and then settle down, round-bellied and content, like a fat sweet seller. The house geckos play statue till a fly hovers, lost, around their heads. Before it can say 'buzz', it is down the lizard's toothless mouth. And of course, there are bigger hunters—kites, mongooses, cats, owls—who grin at the meat chops walking all over the place. *Yum!*

CHIDIYA RANI

Sparrows outnumber them all. Not just during the rains but in all seasons. For many of us, 'bird' immediately means 'sparrow'—the dull brown birdie with buff-and-black stripes, a short tail and a stubby beak, who just melts into the background. Their chirpy little notes are almost an inseparable part of our garden experience. Being the most widely found wild bird on the planet, the sparrow is our model for a bird. This little fellow is actually a power-packed package. The house sparrows spread from the Middle East to the other parts of the world and formed their colonies. They can put the old European colonizers to shame! Humans either took them along as they travelled, or they just hopped on to ships to go on to settle in new lands. Their success is thanks to ours. No less than 10,000 years back, these ordinary-looking birds realized they had to live around humans to grow and be successful. And so, these wild grass-seed eaters followed us where our farming took us, and got used to living with us. Or so the tale goes.

CHATTERBOX

When they are nesting, they tend to get into quarrels easily. These tiny birdies fight with any bird that comes near their nest. It is not a surprise that they are in such a foul mood—a bunch of peckish chicks back home tear their eardrums with their endless and loud demands! The pops and moms shouldn't be complaining, though—they were once the same demanding little babies, weren't they?

The chatty sparrows prefer to live near villages and towns and not in jungles or deserts, away from humans. They are social little beings and never miss their morning and evening sessions of gossip. They gather in flocks and sometimes, their chattering and chirruping rises to a loud pitch. Everyone talks at the same time and each wants to be heard above the din! They prefer to eat together on the ground with family and friends (although they squabble over seeds and grains), roost together, sing together, make their nests in clumps (community housing), and bathe together in water puddles and mud. Mud baths—hmm . . . I bet that's the kind of bath you'd like to try!

TRUTH OR LIE

1. Sparrows like their food served.
2. Sparrows cannot dive underwater.
3. Their name means 'lazy, good-for-nothing birds'.
4. Pox and malaria are deadly sparrow diseases.
5. Pa and ma eat baby sparrows' poop.
6. Sparrow pie is an old European dish.

ANSWERS

1. true

They are used to being served and waited on by us! You must have seen people scattering seeds and grains for sparrows and pigeons. Sparrows mainly eat grains and seeds, although they chomp on a lot of insects and spiders, and even a bit of grit, while growing up. They don't shy away from eating leftovers from our garbage bins either. The delicate girls, in spite of being so little, are dominant in their homes and on feeding grounds. Some even fight noisily over a boy if they happen to like the same one.

Sparrow 1: How dare you smile sideways at my boyfriend, you . . . you brown-tailed buffoon!

Sparrow 2: Hah, why don't you ask him whom he likes better, sis?

2. false

They can. On the ground, they prefer to hop rather than walk. Although they aren't water birds, if sparrows are in danger, they can swim, and even dive, underwater! Though they've adapted well to new environments in the past and are the most widely found birds, in recent years, their population has gone down drastically in many parts of India, and in other countries as well. This is happening because of all the pollution we create and the increasing use of pesticides in our gardens and fields that kill insects—their food. Now, if they have nothing to eat, why would they hang around in our backyards?

In India, some people are fond of feeding sparrows. But some feed them cheap and rotten grains. These grains are full of insecticides (the poison that kills the insects who eat the grain) and that's too much for the little birdies to take.

We've changed our way of living too. In the earlier days, we used to have open spaces and verandas in our houses, where sparrows would make their nests and bring up their families. Now sparrows no longer have those places to build their nests.

On 20 March every year, World Sparrow Day is celebrated. It is to remember the birds who merge so well with our homes that we forget them, even if they go missing from our backyards.

3. nah . . . it doesn't

Their Latin name *P. domesticus* means 'small, active bird that belongs in the house'. When sparrows go to a new place, they can spread about quickly—as far and as fast as 230 km per year! After a day's play and travel, sparrows sleep with their beaks tucked under their feathers, sometimes scratching their little heads with their legs.

The oldest known wild house sparrow died when it was almost twenty years old! The oldest known captive (caged) house sparrow lived to be twenty-three years old. Generally, all animals live much longer in captivity. There are some that live more than double their usual years in cages!

4. oh yes, they are

And sparrows carry a lot of other parasites on them which can spread diseases to other birds too.

5. hard to imagine, but yes

The dad and mum swallow the little ones' poop from the nest for the first few days. After that, they throw it out of the nest. Sparrows generally build their nests in cavities found in walls, tree hollows, hanging lamps in gardens or streetlights, or they simply take up a deserted nest, abandoned by some other bird.

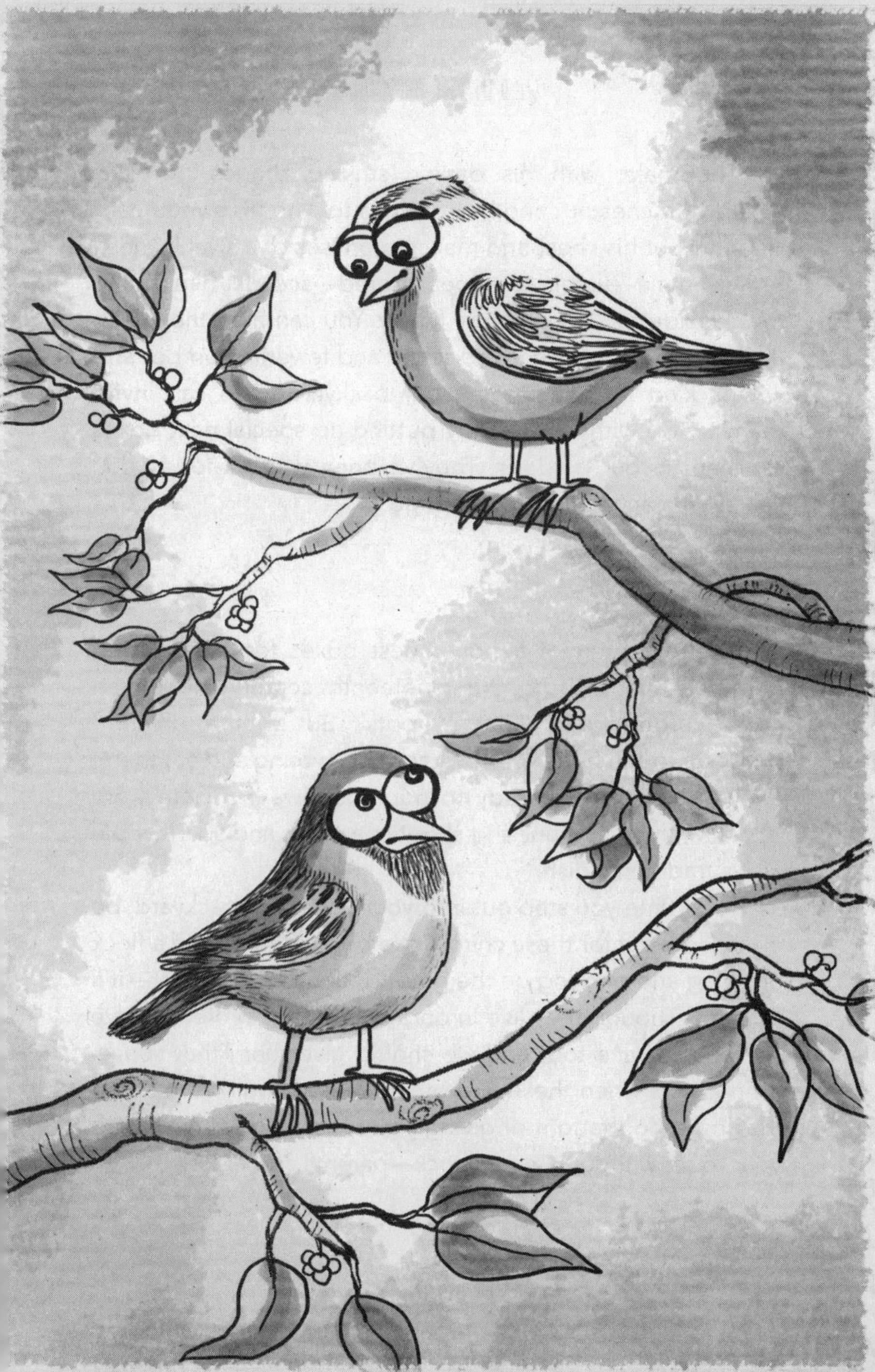

The male, with his darker, striking shades of black mixed with chestnut and brown, tries to woo his sweetheart. He puffs out his chest and makes promises of a swanky nest. If the female—trying to appear bored—accepts him finally, they decide to start a happy family. You can help them with this. Sparrows are becoming fewer and fewer in number and are packing up and leaving our backyards. We can invite them to live with us again by putting up special nest boxes for them in our gardens. They've been with us for 10,000 years! We can't simply let them go.

6. true

Like we're talking of hanging nest boxes for them today, from the sixteenth to the nineteenth century, people in north Europe hung 'sparrow pots'. But with a different purpose: to catch the sparrows and their young and eat them! They also kept nets ready to trap sparrows in. There were 'sparrow clubs' to hunt and shoot sparrows, and sparrow pie was a traditional dish.

Next time you step out into your garden or backyard, be on the lookout for these chirpy little beings. If you find a flock hopping and pecking on the ground, don't go too near—it'll fly away. Though they live in our houses, they prefer to have their own space too, and we should give them that space. Who knows when these two other creatures will learn this— they have no thought of giving you space and just walk into your room without even a knock—parents and ants!

THE
MATEY
MASSES

They don't come by the dozen, they come in hundreds and thousands—marching up and down the walls and floors and gardens and jungles. They climb and gather on your plate to eat the leftovers. They even climb up on you if you're sitting in grass or playing in mud. Even if you've crushed a few and sit there feeling smug, a few more will come and march up your feet as if you are but another stub in the garden. Ants. They are as much a part of your life as the snot in your nose—you can keep digging your nose the whole day but the snot appears again, as if by magic, the next morning!

We've got the following information on ants but there are some words missing. Can you fill in the correct words from the list?

---

pests, waist, queen, colonies, wingless, mounds, drones, tropics, brain, jaws, soldiers, wood

---

Ants are the most social animals after humans. They live in _____ either underground or on trees, or construct _____. The mounds have a maze of rooms inside. Carpenter ants dig in _____ and build their homes there. The colonies can have a few hundred ants or millions of them. The colonies are headed by a _____ who lays thousands of eggs. Sometimes, in super-big colonies, there can be more than one queen. Their societies are divided into classes, like the workers and the _____. The ants that we generally see are the _____ ladies, who are all workers. They do not lay eggs, but gather food (fungus, insects, nectar, seeds), look after the colonies and the queen's children. Every colony has a few _____ (winged males), whose only job is to woo the queen! 12,500 different kinds of ants have been named and there may be 10,000 unnamed ones yet! Ants have strong _____, elbow-shaped antennae and a narrow size-zero _____! They are found almost everywhere on earth, except Antarctica, but most of them love to live in the _____. Their closest relatives are bees and wasps. Not all of them are _____ to humans. We eat them, use them in customs and even for controlling other pests! An ant colony is called a super organism. Why? Because the ants act together as if they have a single _____. What a brainy idea for a story!

ANSWERS

> drones wingless soldiers queen wood mounds colonies
> brain pests tropics waist jaws

THIRTY TERRIBLE AND TERRIFIC TINY TRUTH

1. Ants started farming long before humans! Most ants hunt for or gather food. But a few, like the leaf-cutter ants, grow their own food. They only eat the fungus from their fungal gardens inside their colonies.
   Leaf-cutter ant: Thanks, missy, you can have the grasshopper head. I only eat home-grown, organic food.

2. Most ants are as black as tar or as red as a baboon's bum. But a few are green and some in the tropics sport metallic lustres.
3. Only queens and males have wings. The working females are wingless! How unfair is that!
4. The queen can live up to thirty years! Her age is up to a hundred times longer than any another insect her size living alone! The workers just live about one to three years. What's more, the males only live a few weeks. So much for having those angel wings!
5. Bullet ants have a more painful sting than any other insect! It is not deadly to us, though. But the sting of jack jumper ants can be deadly. And the sting of a fire ant can send you jumping sky-high!
6. Ant Wars: There are some kinds of ants that like to draw blood. They attack their neighbouring ant colonies to feast on their eggs. Or they just steal their eggs and when they hatch, use the captured ants as slaves. The Amazon ants are experts at slave raiding. Except for when they're conducting these raids, they are *so* lazy that they can't even feed themselves and need their slaves to gather their food for them!
7. Ants are useful to humans in more ways than one. They air the soil and make it more fertile. They also control pests. This way, we can avoid using poisonous pesticides. In fact, the farmers in southern China have used weaver ants since 400 BCE to control pests in their citrus orchards. Something we should learn from, so we can invite our sparrows back too!

8. The army ants—the deadly hunters—do not make nests but are always on the move. If there is need for a nest, the workers build it using their own bodies—by holding each other. These moving armies of ants conduct raids and can eat birds, reptiles or even small mammals! A colony of army ants can eat up to 5,00,000 animals in a day!
9. Some worker ants are undertakers—they dispose off their dead nest-mates.
10. A kind of ant found in the Amazon, the *A. decemarticulatus*, is an ambush assassin. It builds leaf traps with holes to catch and kill its prey. Once an insect steps on to it, dozens and dozens of ants catch it with their jaws through the holes!
11. Ants communicate through scent. Ever wondered how one ant comes to a dead insect or a piece of a cake and then hundreds follow? It is because they leave a trail of scent to guide the others. Very Hansel-and-Gretel of them, no?
Ant following trail: That's stink, not scent! When did you bathe—last year?
12. Weaver ants and worker ants build their nest together. The worker ants stand next to each other as a bridge to pull and hold down nest leaves. Then, the weavers quickly use the silk from their larvae to glue the leaves together and build their nest.
13. The trap-jaw ant is a world record holder. It has the fastest snapping jaw on earth—2,300 times faster than the blink of a human eye!
14. Ants' nests can flood during rains. One kind of ant, the *C. muticus*, makes its nest in plant hollows and has a fab

way of protecting its nest. It drinks the water in the nest and goes and pees outside! This is also called communal peeing.
15. Since army ants with their sharp jaws are such deadly killers, humans have found even deadlier ways to use them—not as killers but as healers! Rather than stitching a wound, some doctors in Africa and South America place the army ants on the wound, pressed together. The ants close their jaws on the skin, locking themselves in place. The surgeon then cuts off the rest of the ants' bodies, leaving just the heads locked like stitches on the wound. *Patient: Hey Doc, when do I come to have the stitches—um . . . I mean the beheaded ants—removed?*
16. Some ants form super colonies with more than one queen, and these can stretch for hundreds and thousands of kilometres!
17. Yellow crazy ants from Africa were introduced by mistake on Australia's Christmas Island. It is thought that they accidently climbed ships and arrived on the island somewhere between 1915 and 1930. Known as one of the worst invading species on earth, the yellow crazy ants began to form their super colonies there. At places on Christmas Island, researchers have recorded twenty million ants per hectare! The red crabs, which have always lived on the island, dig burrows and fertilize the forest soil with their poop. They now find it difficult to travel from the forest to the coast once a year. They either lose their way due to the crazy ants or get killed if they pass their nest sites. In the last twenty years, millions of red crabs have been killed by these ants!

18. In Burma and Thailand and some places in India, they serve a special green chutney with their meals—a delicious paste of green weaver ants! Humans eat ants in different parts of the world—making squash-like drinks or pastes, toasting them like peanuts or just squeezing a handful in a fist and having them raw!
19. The *P. sokolova*, found in the swamps of the Australian mangroves, can live underwater. How do these ants without gills breathe easily in their underwater nests? By going about in air bubbles!
20. It is a big effort for the ants living on trees to climb down every time. And so, some have developed special ways to jump down a tree to save time, like the Jerdon's jumping ant does. Others glide down happily, even changing their direction of fall, and choosing their place of landing. *Ant giving advice: Never glide on a full stomach. The gas makes you fly in all the wrong directions. <Burp!>*
21. Lemon ants kill all the plants in an area with their sting, except the lemon ant trees, where they live. This gives them more places to nest, and these clearings are called the 'devil's garden!'
22. Rooibos seeds are used in South Africa to make herbal tea. But the seeds are spread ('dispersed', if you want to sound cool) far and wide by the plants, who want to have more and more baby rooibos plants. Black ants collect these seeds and, clever and lazy as we humans are, we let the ants do all the hard work and collect the piles of rooibos seeds from the ants' nests. We just boil the seeds and sit happily, sipping on their herbal teas.

23. It is not just humans, but even some trees that reap the fruit of the ants' labour: seeds of many trees are spread by ants and the bullhorn acacia tree houses colonies of stinging ants in its hollow thorns as its bodyguards!
Bullhorn acacia: Let's see a pesky goat try and nibble on my leaves!
24. Animals like anteaters and pangolins are, well, ant eaters. They have long, sticky tongues to catch ants with. And strong claws to break the ants' mounds and nests, which can be rock hard! Brown and sloth bears love to dine on ants—They first blow away the dirt and then noisily suck in the ants through the gap in their front teeth. Some researchers have even gone on to find the amount of ant in a brown bear's poop—16 per cent in summer, 12 per cent in spring and 4 per cent in autumn!
25. Some wasps in the tropics, like *M. drewseni*, have learnt how to protect themselves from ant invasion. They use an ant-repellent in their nests. Another kind of wasp, the *A. multipicta*, just throws off the ants from its nest by buzzing its wings at top speed!
26. Many kinds of ants have a sweet tooth. Some colonies even carry along an aphid with them. It's the aphid that eats plant sap and makes honeydew—the ants' favourite dessert!
27. Different kinds of ants form give-and-take friendships with different insects, plants and fungi. However, there are some animals that prefer to eat ants rather than be chummy with them, including certain kinds of fungi! The fungus *C. unilateralis* first infects the ant, which causes

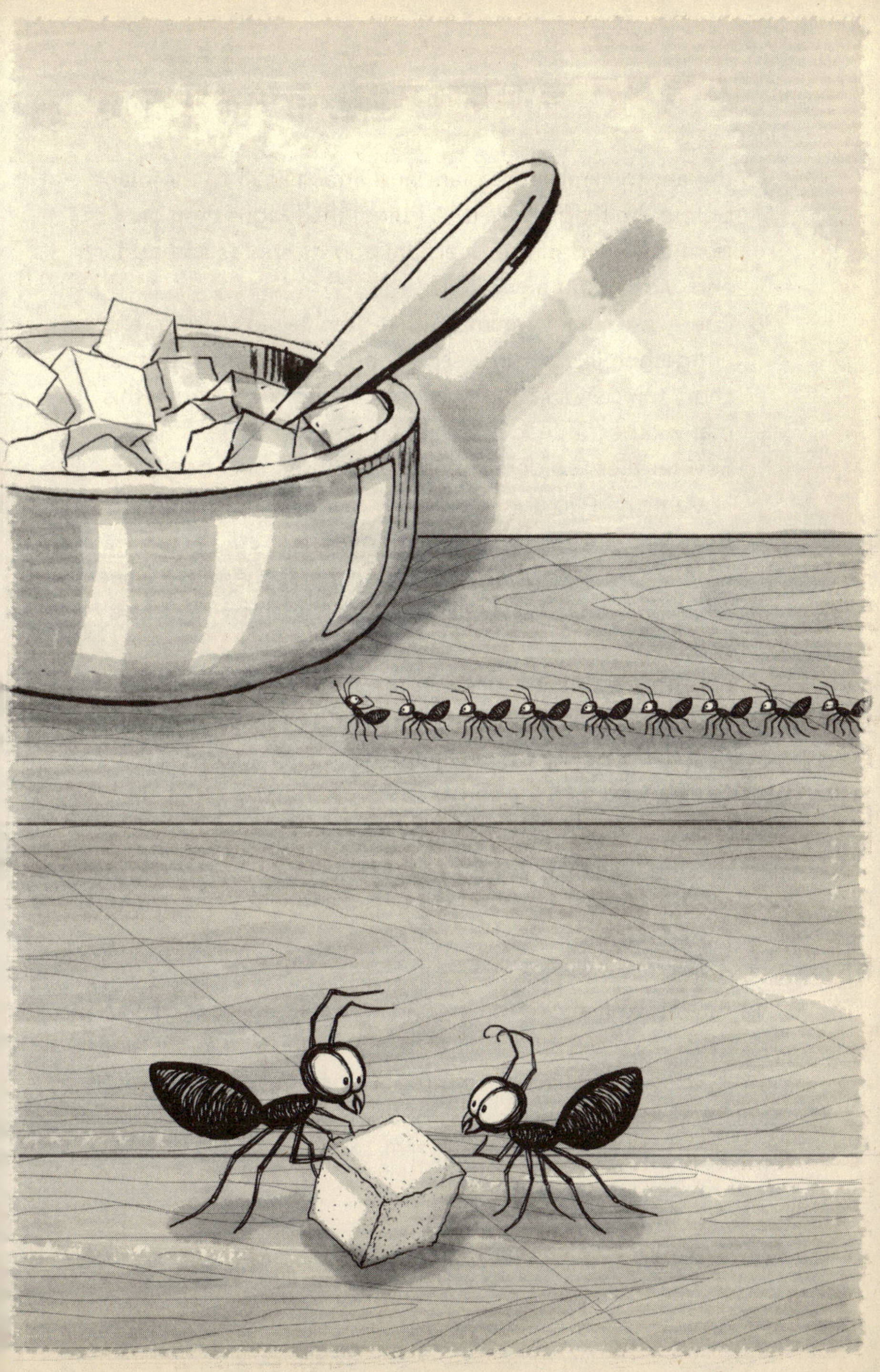

the ant to climb up a plant and attach itself to the plant before the fungus kills it. A fruit of the fungus then grows from the head of the dead ant and its spores spread far and wide. What a way to breed!

28. There are many animals that just avoid eating ants altogether, like some wasps and birds, because of their short temper and nasty stings. Taking a cue from this, many other little critters mimic ants to avoid hunters! Several flies, spiders, beetles, mantises and bugs look like ants and go about their day-to-day work smugly.
Boy: Mama, the bug boy says I'm a copycat!
Mama: Oh no, darling, you're a copy-ant! And we'll see what bug boy has to say after the sparrow flies away with him!

29. How many ants are there in the world anyway, you ask? Between one and ten quadrillion! (10,000,000,000,000,000!) And don't ask me who counted them. I'm finding it difficult to even count all the zeros here.

30. Here's a simpler way to understand it: They say the total weight of all the ants on earth is equal to the total weight of all humans. One million ants for one human being! Go figure!

Ants are at work above the ground (not the queen, of course, who rests royally in her hidden chambers) and below our feet, in the dark depths where the roots go about silently doing their work. There is a creature of the night living around our homes in the tall trees that is as difficult to glimpse as ants are easy to spot. Whooooo is that?

THE
SILENT
KILLER

There are so many times we hear people say, 'I wish I were a bird.' When we think of birds, we only think of wings. And flying. And no homework. Being a bird is not just fluttering your wings. Or dreaming happily as you glide over cliffs and oceans. It can also mean fighting for survival—killing or becoming someone's dinner! (And, of course, it also means getting fleas in your feathers.)

Now, this bird that lives in those tall trees around our homes is a mystery to many. Its eyes are always open wide in surprise, as if it has just seen a ghost. For all we know, it probably has, as it is generally up and about in the dark hours of the night! A bird of prey, with a straight back, broad head, curved, pointed beak and flat face, the owl sits on the dark branches of the trees around our homes, hidden in the black cloak of night. The one that is the most common around our homes is the spotted owlet. There are some owls that come out at dusk or dawn, but most hunt in complete darkness.

Owls, all the 200-plus kinds, have super senses. Let's take a look, shall we?

EYES OF THE WISE

The 200 kinds of owls are divided into two families. One is the true owl. Which is the other? No, not the false owl—the barn owl. You can tell a barn owl apart from a true owl by its heart-shaped face.

Owls have flat faces and two forward-facing, button-like eyes that help them to see extremely well in the dark.

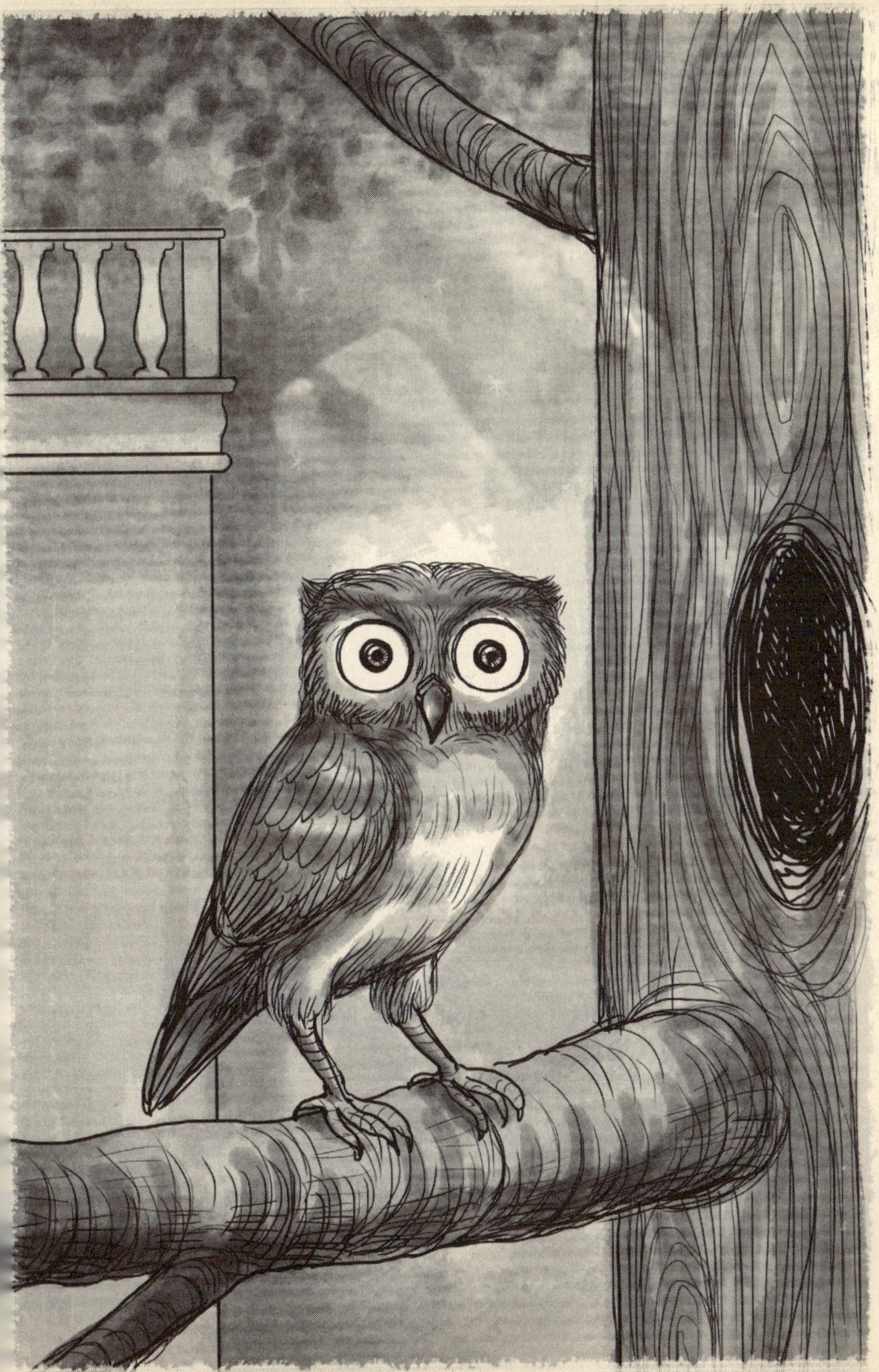

They have a disk of feathers, called a facial disk, around each eye, and it makes them look like they are wearing round spectacles to match their famed wisdom!

The eyes of the owl are unlike those of most other birds of prey, who have eyes on either side of their face. This gives them binocular-like vision—they can see far-off things clearly, but not those nearby. This makes owls far-sighted . . . No wonder they are considered wise!

Oodles of Owly Myth

Athena, the goddess of wisdom in ancient Greece, had the symbol of an owl. Though the owl was considered wise in many western cultures, in Finnish culture, it was considered an idiot. The Finnish word *pöllö* means both 'owl' and 'fool'.

EERIE EARS

Owls have holes for ears. The facial disk we talked about earlier funnels the sounds to the earholes, making them hear louder and clearer. Both the earholes can be different in size! This helps them to pinpoint a sound, even if is the slight rustle of a rat under the leaves. It's the ears that do the real hunting.

The great Indian horned owl, or the eagle owl, has two pointed ears like the horns of a devil. But they are not ears at all; they are just pointed feather tufts. (Too bad! You'd rather they were the horns of a devil, wouldn't you?)

AREFA TEHSIN

Oodles of Owly Myth

The great Indian horned owl or the eagle owl is one of the two heaviest- and largest-winged owls of the world—its wings can spread as wide as 6.6 ft! In India, they are used in dark magic and witchcraft rituals—some sillies use owl flesh to cast curses; other loonies capture and sacrifice these poor owls on the moonless night of Diwali to obtain the philosopher's stone, which, they believe, they hide in their nests. If only those crazies realized that they were killing the poor things for nothing but owl poop.

THE SILENT HUNTERS

A group of owls is called a parliament, though they prefer to live alone. It does seem they're not pea-brained enough to have an actual parliament—unlike us. They can well manage their own affairs, thank you very much.

Owls are found all over the earth except Antarctica. They hunt small mammals, birds and insects. A few hunt fish too. No big deal, you say? Try hunting fish or even an insect with your bare hands. And that too in the dark!

What is it that makes them such posh night hunters?

Crafty Colour: Why do you think owls are so difficult to spot? Because their dull colours blend with the surroundings and make them almost invisible.

Fantastic Flight: Their flight is silent, and not flappy and noisy like the eagles'. They descend to the ground, almost invisible on their silent wings. And then fly away with a squeaking rat or squirrel in their mouths to kingdom come.

Terrible Talons: The owls then crush their prey with their powerful talons—skull, tail and all.

Beastly Beak: The beak that curves downward and is pointed, like a hawk's, tears the prey apart and gulps it down—scales, fur, all of it. Not picky at all!

Since it eats up the whole prey, the owl finds it hard to digest some of the things it swallows. And so it has to throw it out from its mouth in the form of small pellets. You might even get an owl pellet to dissect in your biology class! You can find out from that little piece what the owl had for dinner.

Oodles of Owly Myth

The Kikuyu of Kenya, and many old cultures of North and South America, believe that owls bring death, misery and destruction. There is an old saying in Mexico: 'When the owl cries, the Indian dies.'

THEIR FAVOURITE PASTIME: RATTING, OF COURSE!

They say that for every man in India, there are six rats. And six rats eat one man's food!

Breed a pair of rats in ideal conditions for one year. By the end of the year, there'll be so many rats that if we placed them one above the other, they would reach all the way up to the moon!

Rats destroy foodgrains and spread diseases like the plague. Now, a happy and hungry barn owl family can eat up to 3000 rats in one nesting season. You can keep an owl nest box in your garden and boast to your friends about the mysterious bird that lives in your backyard!

HECK, DON'T CRANE YOUR NECK!

Owls can turn their necks up to 270 degrees! Since their eyes are fixed in the sockets, they need to move their heads to look around. Imagine the girl sitting in front of you in class turning her neck, without turning her body, to ask, 'Hey, did you do your biology homework?' As if the mention of homework were not spooky enough!

Oodles of Owly Myth

In India, the owl is considered the steed of Goddess Lakshmi.

MAD MIMICRY

The great Indian horned owl is a fantastic mimic. It can imitate a variety of sounds, including human speech. It has led people to believe in ghosts by crying or laughing in the dead of night. Or by just imitating what you say.

You: Who's there?
Owl: Whooooo's there?
Well, that's enough to wet your pants, I'd say!

Oodles of Owly Myth

In India, it is believed that if an owl sits on your roof and imitates the sound of a crying baby, you're in deep trouble. But if it just silently sits there all night, then something good is about to happen. Like your school closing due to heavy rains!

These silent killers go about their nightly routine without disturbing us. But if we try and get too familiar with them, they will naturally attack. This can happen especially when an owl is with its screaming babies—I mean, the poor bird already has enough to worry about! The famous wildlife photographer Eric Hosking lost one of his eyes to a tawny owl when he tried to photograph it. His autobiography is called *An Eye for a Bird*. Wouldn't we do the same if an owl came too near us to check us out?

There is one animal that lurks on our walls and checks us out all the time, though. Whether we're picking our noses or just sitting quietly in the bathroom doing our thing. Who's this creep?

WALL-G

It sits stock-still on your walls, tilting its head sometimes to look at you. In a rare instance, it can slip from the wall and land on your head with a plop. Now, that sure can send you screaming down the hall.

Gecko: Look at the loony go! And I thought I had the bone-rattling fall!

Geckos are colourful lizards who prefer to live in warm places all over the world *(Gecko: Nothing like a balmy day, my sweet)*—in rainforests, deserts, jungles, grasslands, cities and even cold mountain slopes. There is a wide range of geckos—no less than 1,500 different kinds! Although you may find one looking down, don't expect it to bat its eyelids at you. Because they don't have any. Eyelids, I mean. So they lick the transparent skin on their eyeballs, one at a time, to keep them clean and moist. Don't think that's impressive? Try reaching your eyes with your tongue. It won't even reach your nose!

I bet your teacher loves geckos. Why don't you go and impress her with these gawky gecko facts?

1. Dogs may curl their tails and run, geckos may leave their tails and run! Geckos use their tails to balance themselves when they climb. They also store fat in them to use later. But the swankiest is when they simply leave their tails behind when under attack. If one tries to catch a gecko, it'll shed its tail and scat. (The fancy term for this tail-leaving is 'autotomy'.) And the tail will keep twitching for a while to fool the hunter. The hunter can't make out the telltale signs!

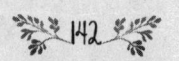

2. Most geckos, including our house geckos, come out at night. You'd probably find them sitting beady-eyed near the light on the porch. Or near the tube light of your bedroom. Certain geckos can see colours in dim light. What do *we* see in dim light? Mostly black and white. That is why they say the colour vision of these geckos is 350 times better than ours! What do you think would be the names of *all* the colours they can see? Violet, *Zylot*, Green, *Breen*, Blue, *Kuyoo* . . . phew! Colours we probably won't *ever* have names for!
3. Geckos mainly eat insects and worms. But some large geckos can kill and eat even small birds, reptiles and mammals like mice. That is why they are welcomed in some homes, especially since they eat mosquitoes as well. They are considered housecleaners. These geckos don't get canned spiders and ready-to-pop mosquitoes in supermarkets and so they hunt them in our homes and eat them raw. Do you know, some people even keep geckos as pets in glass boxes!
    The geckos, in turn, are eaten by a lot of animals—big spiders, snakes, birds, and mammals like cats. Some kinds of geckos can be quite colourful, though the house gecko is a bit dull.
    House Gecko: Who are you calling dull, huh? Have a look at your skin, mate!
4. Many geckos can climb walls and other upright structures. They even walk upside down on the ceiling! They have special toes that stick like suction pads to the surface. Their feet also self-clean as they walk. The sucker feet

stick even better on wet surfaces, however, their feet lose their stickiness if they're completely inside water. If they lose their grip and fall on your head, don't worry, they won't bite. House geckos are harmless. Even if a larger one tries to bite, it will not be able to penetrate your skin. By the way, geckos can replace each one of their near-hundred teeth once every few months. They might look toothless, like your grandma or baby brother, but they're not!

Scientists are trying to study how geckos walk on straight walls and ceilings. Very soon, you might have a cool machine to climb smooth, vertical surfaces, just like geckos do! Maybe they'll call it the Gecko-Man or the Gecko-Girl.

5. Geckos are very talkative lizards. They chirp and they bark. Usually, they make a clicking sound, *tchak-tchak-tchak*, three times when they are trying to find a lover. And they continue clicking as they go towards their sweetheart's arms. This little lizard's bullhorn-like voice can make you jump from your bed. Its name 'gecko' itself comes from the Malaysian word *gēko*, which is the sound that it makes.

6. The mama gecko generally lays two sticky eggs, and usually in piles of leaves or the barks of trees. Inside the house, they find some quiet places to lay their eggs. Like inside your cricket gloves hanging on that wall, untouched for so long. Don't worry, the mama doesn't hang around to look after her little ones once they hatch. You won't find her creeping up your hand when you decide to put on your gloves the next time you go playing cricket!

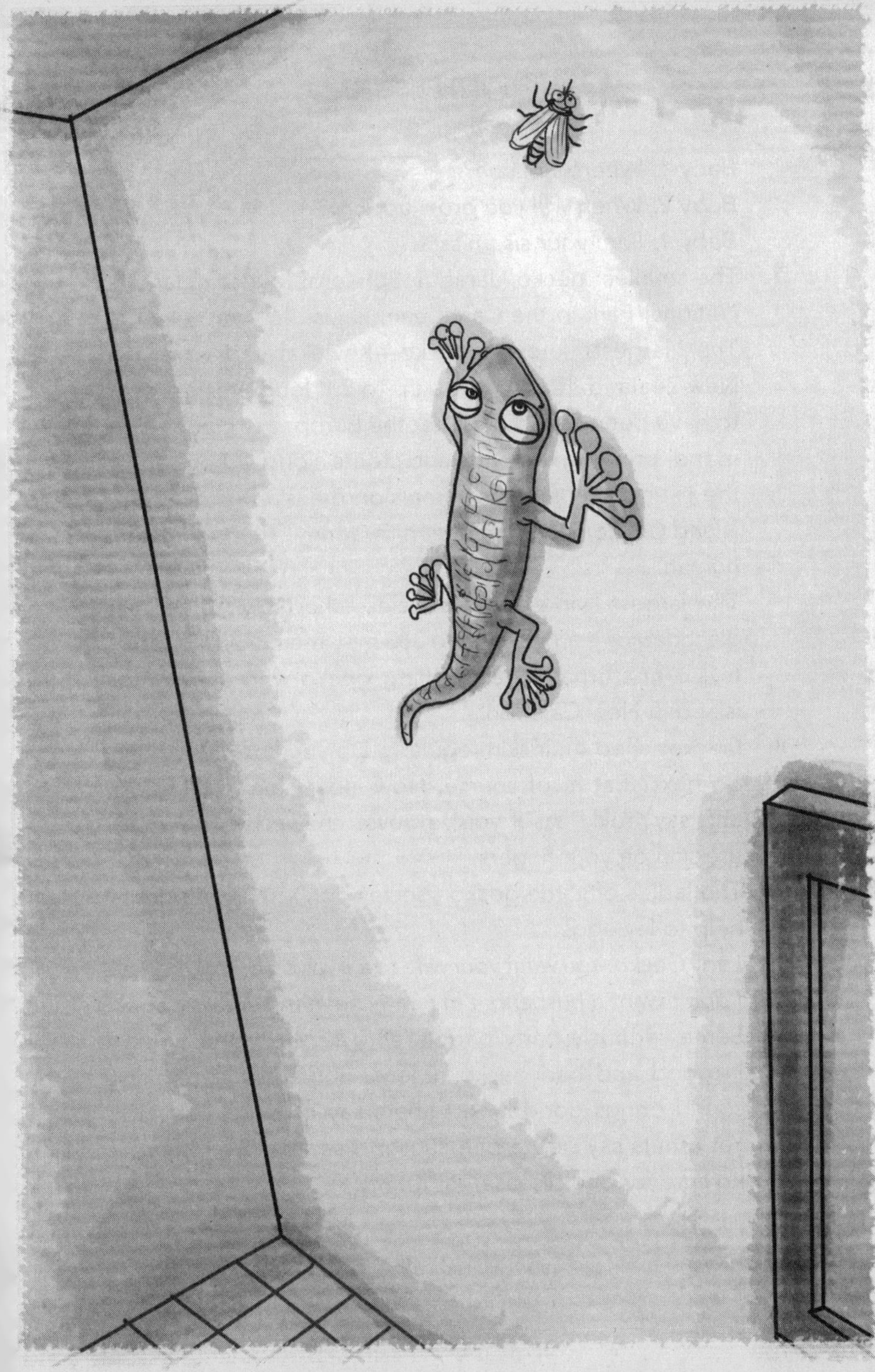

Baby 1: Where's mama?
Baby 2: When will you grow up, bro?
Baby 1: I am your sis, miss!

7. The smallest gecko, Jaragua Sphaero, found in Jaragua National Park in the Caribbean, is just 16 mm in length. The largest known gecko—Kawekaweau—lived in New Zealand. It used to be up to 2 ft long! It is believed to have been wiped out after the Europeans came to the island, bringing their rats and stoats along—they caused the extinction of many animals on the island.

   Island Gecko: Don't go near him, sonny! That's a horrible human.

   The largest living gecko species—the New Caledonian giant gecko—can grow up to 360 mm (more than 1 ft long!). It is a nocturnal, tree-dwelling gecko who lives on an island in New Caledonia.

8. Geckos shed their skin regularly. Do you know what they do next? Eat it, of course. Now, now, don't pull a face and say 'Yuck!' As if you've never chewed your nails or the skin on your fingers!

9. The ladies of some gecko species don't need the gents' help to lay eggs.

   Lady Gecko: You want your wife to serve you dinner, honey? I don't want a husband. I'm not living in the Jurassic age!

10. Some seriously batty people all over the world believe in good and bad gecko omens. Some say its clicking sound brings good luck. Others say it brings bad luck. Yet others say gecko pee causes diseases. Well, there is no cure for one disease—stupidity.

AREFA TEHSIN

If your teacher is not impressed by you rattling off your gawky gecko facts, try giving her your beloved pet gecko. If she still lets out a cry of horror, you can tell her all about this critter who lives in your garden trees. There is hardly anyone who wouldn't like to see this cuddly, furry animal playing around and looking all cute.

THE SHADOW-TAILED

You'll hardly find anyone who hasn't seen a squirrel. They would have either seen the 10-cm-long African pygmy squirrel or the 3-ft-long Indian giant squirrel. Or any of the more than 200 varieties in-between. They dart around home gardens, city parks, woodlands and jungles. You wouldn't want to think that these cute, furry creatures are in any way related to rats, now, would you!

Squirrels are rodents. Their name means 'shadow tailed'— because of their bushy tails, of course. Oh well, almost all names have meanings. We've cleverly named ourselves *Homo sapiens* (*Homo* = man + *sapiens* = wise). And named others 'shadow-tailed' or 'river horse' (hippo = horse + potamus = river) or 'Dracula' (is that what you call your school principal?).

SQUEAKY SQUIRRELS

Squirrels are found naturally in Asia, Europe, the Americas and Africa, but not in Australia, where they were introduced by humans. They have silky fur, padded paws, bushy tails and large, wonder-struck eyes. We usually see tree squirrels scampering from branch to garden wall to tree trunk. Some squirrels live in tunnels and burrows. They may even sleep in these tunnels for the whole of winter. If you remember, the fancy word for this long winter sleep is 'hibernation'.

The squirrel family includes:

- tree squirrels
- ground squirrels
- flying squirrels

- chipmunks
- marmots
- prairie dogs

Yes, prairie dogs are squirrels, not dogs. And flying squirrels don't fly, they glide. It's going to be an exercise in futility if we start wondering why people give such confusing names!

Prairie dogs are chubby squirrels that live on the ground and are found in North America. The squirrels that live on the ground are more social than the ones that live on trees. Most squirrels are active during the day and sleep at night, but the flying squirrels are creatures of the night and that's when they come out of their tree hollows.

This reminds me of a real life ghost story; it's a ghost story Dr Raza had heard time and again: The story is set in the thick jungles of Sitamata in Rajasthan. In the old days, there used to be a thriving village there, called Arampura. This village was destroyed three times by the plague—a deadly disease. The third time, it was utterly ruined. Slowly, the jungle took over this village and the only reminder of the tragedy was a well.

The villagers and the locals of that jungle believed that a flying spirit rose up from that well every night, and it was said that if it flew over your head, you would get married . . . Nah! (That would be quite another horror, though, wouldn't it? Or would it be a fairy tale then? Anyway, that's not part of *this* story!) They said if it flew over your head, you would die.

Raza decided to get to the bottom of this superstition and went on this mission with his dad, his brother and his friend,

WILD IN THE BACKYARD

a forest officer. They camped in the jungles of Sitamata and started their hunt for the deadly flying spirit. For many days and nights, they scanned the forest with the help of a forest dweller. However, the ghost was too clever for them.

Guess what happened when they finally lost heart and decided to come back home? At dusk, the spirit rose from its sleep and flew right over their heads!

You want to know who the ghost was? The large brown flying squirrel!

It is almost 3 ft, from head to tail, and looks like a black kite in flight. The part of its skin between its feet stretches and spreads out while it flies and remains folded when it walks. No wonder the people of the area believed it was a cloaked dark spirit of the night. This was the first time a large brown flying squirrel was discovered in that area.

Well, whether it was a squirrel or a spirit from the underworld, Raza didn't get married after that (though that could probably have something to do with the fact that he was already married) nor did he die. That is how we know the tale.

The End

Here are a few questions about squirrels. Four of the five answers are correct. Can you tell which the incorrect one is?

1. Squirrels eat:
   a. nuts, roots, seeds, plants
   b. baby birds and baby snakes
   c. fallen-off teeth of animals

    d. eggs, insects, caterpillars
    e. tree sap and fungi
2. Squirrels live in:
    a. rainforests
    b. Delhi
    c. Mumbai
    d. the driest of deserts
    e. snow
3. Squirrels are:
    a. clever
    b. hoarding creatures
    c. vocal and loud
    d. easily tamed
    e. meek and calm

ANSWERS

1. c. fallen-off teeth of animals

This was an easy one. Squirrels mostly eat nuts, plants and other vegetable matter. Sometimes, they also catch and eat insects, eggs and baby birds. You can sit out on your porch in the rains and observe—that's the time when a lot of delicious flying insects and creepy-crawlies come out. Squirrels love to feast on them. You might find a busy squirrel catching flying insects, plucking their wings and crunching them raw. They might even have some caterpillar pulp to make their snack a bit saucy.

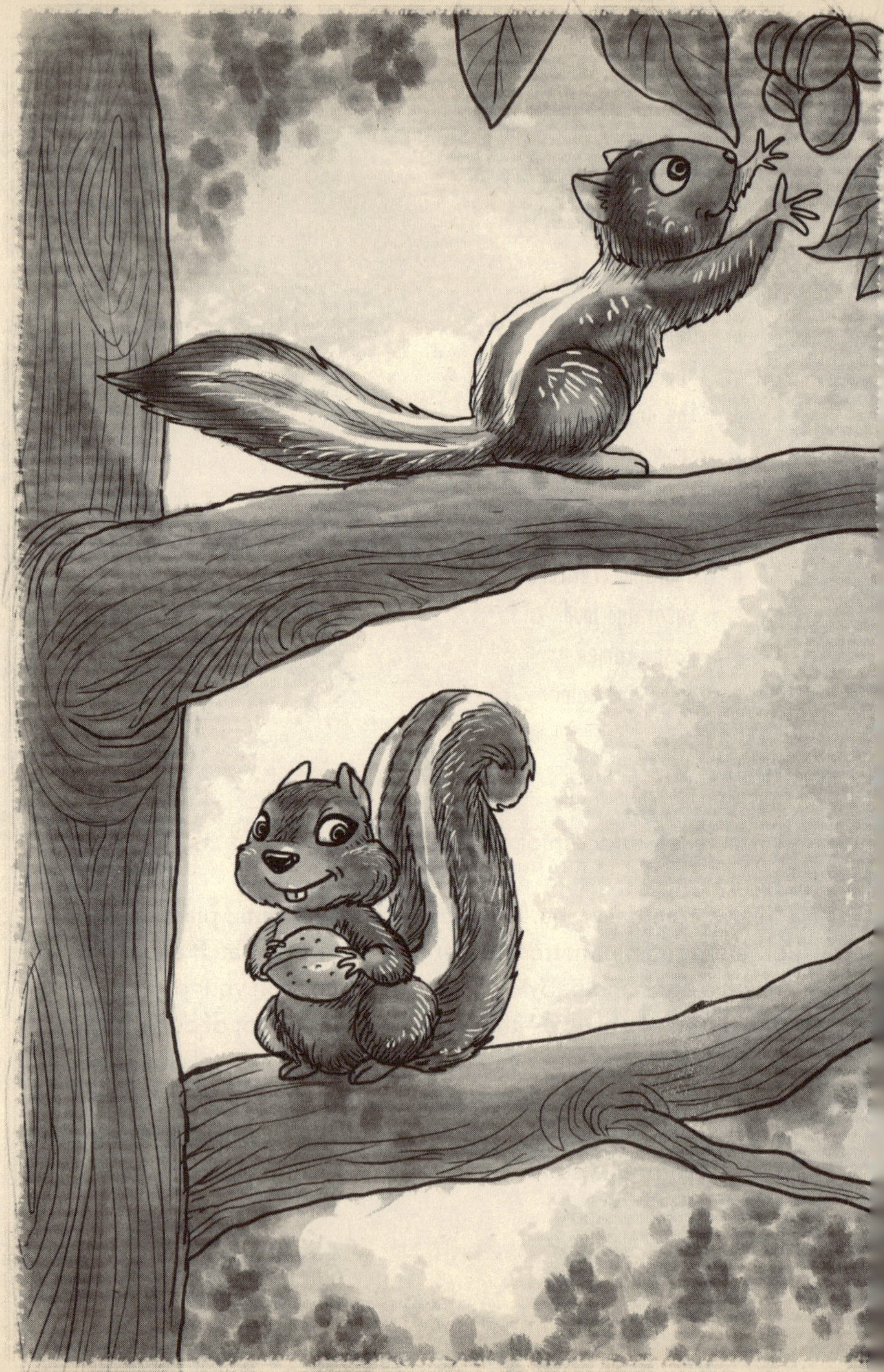

Squirrels living in colder climates gather food supplies for winter. When the red squirrel of the US runs low on nuts gathered for winter, it goes to the sugar maple trees. It scratches the bark of the maple with its teeth and leaves the sap to trickle. Once it is dry and sticky on the bark, our squirrel returns to lick its maple-syrup lollypop!

Many animals like to eat the tender meat of squirrels. That is why most baby squirrels are eaten in their first year. If they survive, they can live about five to ten years in the wild. If they are zoo squirrels, they can live for almost double the number of years.

2. d. the driest of deserts

Squirrels are found almost everywhere but they avoid the very dry deserts as well as the high altitude regions of the poles. In India, the most common ones are the two that live on trees—the five-striped squirrels and the three-striped squirrels. The first one lives in north India and the second in south India. They build football-sized nests with all the cosy things they can gather—cotton, cloths, twigs, grass, etc. Their nests—dreys—are super-comfy chambers. These two (the five- and the three-striped) squirrels do not hibernate in the winter.

There is a story behind the five stripes on this squirrel. When Lord Rama, with his army of monkeys, was building a bridge across the sea to Lanka to rescue the kidnapped Sita, a little squirrel came and helped too. Pleased, Rama stroked the squirrel's back and the marks of his fingers remained on the squirrel, giving it its stripes.

3. e. meek and calm

Squirrels are all but quiet and calm.

They go *chip-chip-chip* in their loud, sharp voices and twitch their tails with jerks to warn the others. They can fight like the aunty next door when your ball lands on her porch—by mistake, of course! They get really angry if a bird or another squirrel tries to approach the food they've collected, and they fight loudly—you can be woken from your afternoon slumber by their squealing squirrel fights.

It's easily possible to tame them too. If you offer them food, that is. They'll come and take food from your hands and then squat on the ground near you. They'll hold the morsel in both their hands and nibble away at it. Their cute front four teeth never stop growing throughout their lives, so the teeth don't wear down from all the nibbling. These cute furry creatures, however, can be a real bother as well. You will realize this if you're trying to put up a bird feeder—they always find a way to eat the food you've kept for the birds!

And doesn't this show they are super clever? They are quite protective of their food. The grey squirrel, found in the US, pretends to bury a nut in order to fool the bird or another squirrel watching it. The thief comes to get this fake buried nut, while the squirrel goes and buries its real nut elsewhere!

A frantic robin to his angry lady as he digs with his beak: Sweetheart, I swear I remember the burial site correctly!

Stashing away food for future use is called hoarding. Many squirrels do it, but the five-striped and the three-striped squirrels found in India don't hoard, since they get enough food all year round. Many times, squirrels forget where they've buried their nuts or acorns, and so we have many new trees grow from these forgotten nuts! These clever squirrels end up planting big, wondrous trees for us. They might look at the tree growing and think later to themselves, 'So this is what happened to my best walnut, huh?'

Squirrels, with their big, round eyes have excellent eyesight. But these other creatures living with us in our homes are happily blind.

THE UNTAMED SHREW

Yes, this is a shrew that can't be tamed. Do you know the shrew that *can* be tamed? Oh, never mind. Only Mr Shakespeare can answer that. Or you can even try asking your dad, 'Have you tamed the shrew?' Just make sure you ask this question standing at the door, ready to run. You'll need to if your mum hears this!

Shrews look like long-nosed mice. But don't confuse them with rats. They are not rodents—which means they are not related to rats or mice. They have sharp teeth, which are not like the two cute bunny-teeth of rats. Unlike the front teeth of rats, the shrews' teeth do not grow throughout their lives. Shrews lose their milk teeth before they're born. They have only one set of teeth all their lives. So there's no shrew tooth fairy.

The ones that are found in and around houses in India are the Asian house shrews. They are the biggest shrews in the world. They're 15 cm long. If *that's* the biggest, what is the smallest? The smallest is the Etruscan shrew, which is just 3.5 cm long and weighs as little as 2 g! It is the smallest land mammal.

BALDY BELIEF

It is believed in some parts of India that if a shrew runs over your head, you will turn bald.

Wife: Darling, you're going bald.

Husband: A shrew ran over my head . . . hee . . . haw . . . haw! Um . . . I didn't mean you, honey. Oh dear . . . I'm dead.

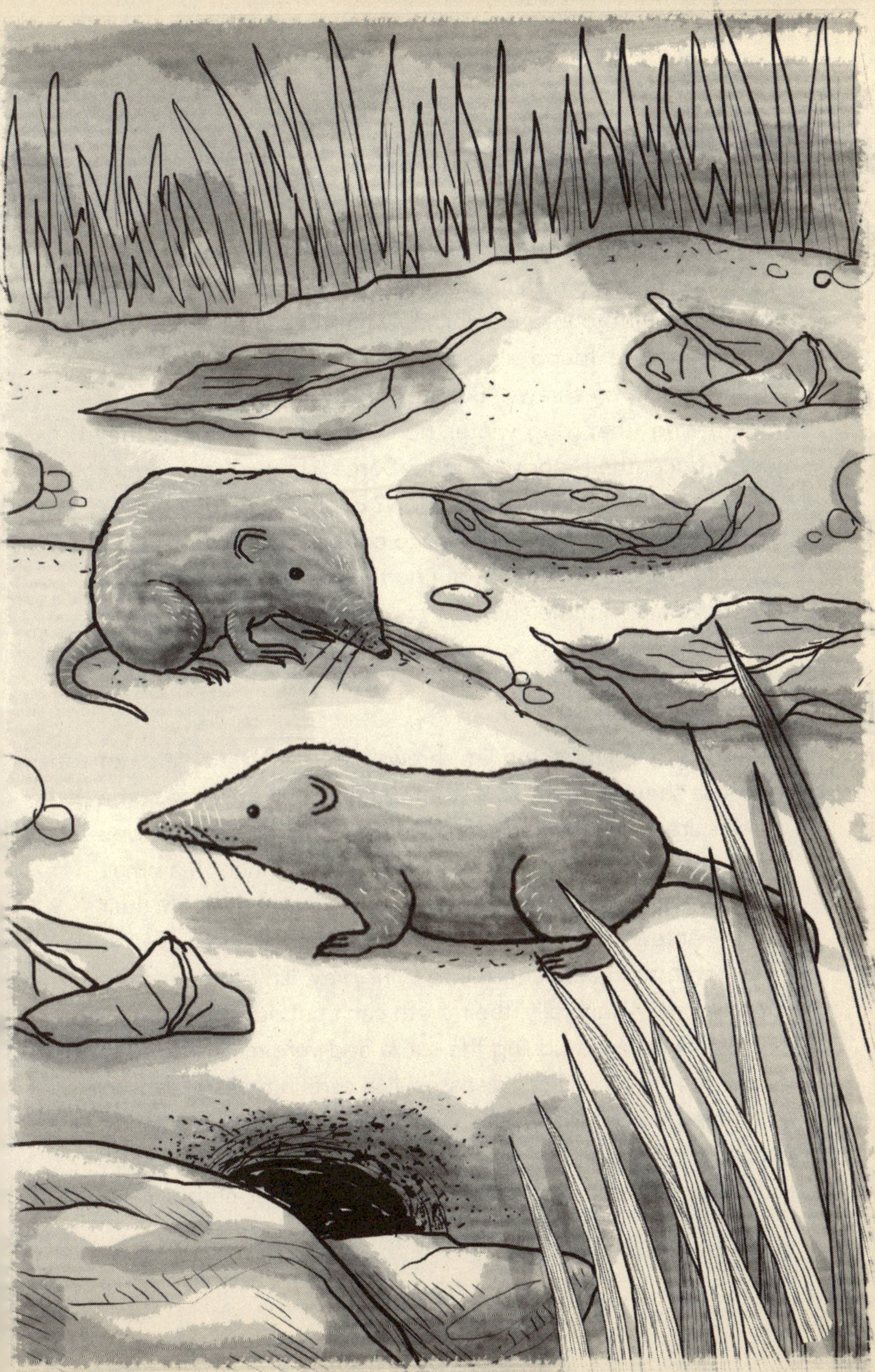

WILD IN THE BACKYARD

DR SHREW'S CLINIC: LOSE WEIGHT BY LOSING BRAIN

Are you a bit chubby and want to get rid of the double chin? Think again. Double chins are cute. Even after thinking again, if you still want to lose weight, do what the shrew does.

Shrews are found almost all over the world. There are 385 varieties of shrews! But in the cold areas, instead of hibernating (that long winter sleep we talked about?) they just reduce their body weight. Some shrews can reduce 30–50 per cent of their weight! How? By shrinking their bones, skulls and organs. Simple! Want to consider doing that? I bet you'll turn and say, 'Thanks, but no thanks. I'm happy with my brain size and double chin.'

TERRIFIC TEETH

Scientists are interested in shrews' teeth and no, it's not because they're the shrews' tooth fairies. It is because some shrews are venomous! It is rare for a mammal to have venom. The American short-tailed shrew is one such mammal. They are not like snakes, who inject venom through their fangs—shrews don't *have* fangs. They use the grooves in their teeth to inject venom into their prey. Isn't that groovy? Don't worry—generally, their teeth can't cut our skin.

Scientists are studying the saliva and venom of shrews to find cures for a lot of our diseases, like certain types of cancer.

Being a scientist is hard work. It can take *years* to study something in *so* much detail. Oops! Did the word 'study' just put you off? But really, it's pretty cool, actually—scientists make some really neat discoveries. Like finding out about the super-big craters on the moon and opening up stomachs of mummies to see what is stuffed inside. Wouldn't you just love to do that?

SWANKY SHREWS

Shrews love to munch on nuts and worms, seeds and insects and other such yummies. Most kinds of shrews live on the ground. A few are experts at climbing trees. There are some that even live under snow or underground. And then there are water shrews! They live near water and hunt in water as well. They trap air bubbles in their fur in order to swim. No, the air bubbles are not their farts. In case you were wondering! These air bubbles are their floats.

Shrews are hungry little critters. They can eat half to twice their body weight every day! They can hear and smell very well too. After all, they have Pinocchio-like noses. However, they can hardly see. Having the eyesight of a hundred-year-old nanny doesn't bother some kinds of shrews. A few of them can also echolocate like bats. (Remember we read how bats fly using their echoes in the dark?) They locate things in the dark with their echoes. Even some toothed whales do that inside water!

MONEY SHREW

The money shrew is actually the Asian house shrew. This is the most common shrew found in backyards in India. It makes a sound just like the jingling of coins as it runs. That's why it is called the money shrew in China. There is an even more interesting name for this shrew—*chachunder*.

Grey-brown-bodied, hairy-tailed, with a long nose and five clawed toes, the *chachunder* has a terrible smell. It is not the smell of their pee or poop, it is just their style statement. And it increases when they have to find a partner.

Lady Shrew: My . . . do you smell!
Shrew Stud: Nothing but the best for you, baby.

The *chachunder* comes out at night from its hidden home—it can be inside your house or in your garden. When it is inside the house, it moves along the edges of the walls, and cats and other predators leave it well alone. Would *you* care to eat a dish that smelled awful? It's not just the smell that is terrible—the house shrew's cry, when it's upset, is like nails scratching a chalkboard! Cats keep their distance from this loud-mouthed, horrid-smelling creature.

FOLLOW ME!

The *chachunder* has an interesting habit. The little ones form a train behind their mother when she goes for a stroll. Or grocery shopping. The first kid holds the mum's fur with its teeth. The second holds the brother or sister before it . . . and so on. The train or caravan of the *chachunder* mum with her kids is fun to watch. Don't you also do the same when you go out with your mum or dad—hold their hands?

Many people just let them be in their house as they are not harmful. In fact, they eat cockroaches and even mice, and keep our homes pest free. Do you know, the elephant shrew found in Africa can jump like a hare? It uses its back legs for the long jumps. Can you think of another creature in our backyard that is a jolly jumper?

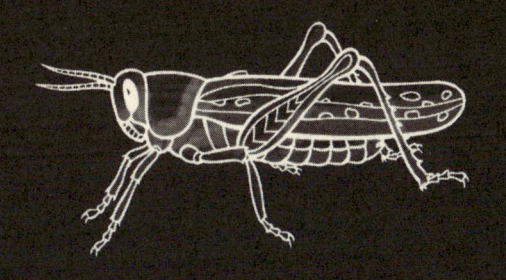

THE HOPPER GANGS

No, they don't always operate in gangs. When they do, these hopping vegetarians can be deadlier than snakes and scorpions put together. When thousands or millions of them form a gang, we call them locusts and when they live alone in our gardens and meadows, we call them grasshoppers. And what do they call us? The hopeless . . . um . . . hop-less giants, maybe?

With their heads bent at an angle, grasshoppers look stern. These insects can smell and touch things with their antennae. Their hind legs have claws and are very strong. Grasshoppers don't need a violin or a guitar to make music—they have pegs in their hindlimbs, which they rub with their forewings to play a tune. The boys sing for the girls. Crickets, who are cousins of grasshoppers, also do the same. They are strictly vegetarian and love to chew their grass-and-leaf meal. But some of them eat flesh and animal poop at times too.

THE JOLLY JUMPERS

Grasshoppers don't only jump. They fly as well! They jump to go from one place to the next to escape a smart guy planning to eat them for supper, or when they are surprised. Scientists have listed no less than 11,000 kinds of grasshoppers. And there are many more that we don't know about. Many of the ones we don't know of live in wet tropical forests. Do you know that one tree of a tropical rainforest has hundreds of different animals living in it? Many of these animals have not even been discovered yet, and we just chop down one huge, gorgeous tree, home to so many animals, to make a lounge chair. Really, I mean.

HOPPER HORROR STORIES

Egg Me Not: Grasshoppers are eaten by many animals. The mum lays the eggs in pods on the ground. She then buries them in the soil or under leaf litter. A few mums stick the eggs together with froth. (Tip: Gather a lot of saliva in your mouth. Then mix it with a few air bubbles and bring it out. There! You have your froth.) But hiding the eggs doesn't always help—some beetles and bee-flies manage to locate the eggs and eat them sunny side up.
Hoppers for Starters: Spiders, wasps, robber flies, lizards, ants, other insects and birds, all gorge on grasshoppers. And So. Do. We.

Fried, Toasted or Sun-dried?

Have you tasted one? You can try it with tortilla in chilli sauce as some south Mexicans do. Or go to China to eat it served on skewers (spikes used for cooking). If you want to have boiled, salted and sun-dried ones, you'll have to go to the Middle East. If you like it fried (I wouldn't recommend fried stuff, though), you'll have to visit Indonesia. And according to the Bible, John the Baptist ate locusts and wild honey in the wilderness.

Pitiless Parasites: Grasshoppers have parasites too, like blowflies and flesh flies. But the real heartless ones are a few others that we'll now take a look at.

- There's a hair worm that dictates the behaviour of the grasshopper. It lives inside the hopper's body and makes the grasshopper jump into the water and drown itself! The parasite then comes out of the grasshopper's body, three times longer than the hopper, and swims away to find a mate!
- There is a long, slender worm called a grasshopper nematode. It lays its eggs on the leaves that grasshoppers eat. And once it is inside the grasshopper's body, it feeds on what the grasshopper eats. When it is ready to face the world, it comes out of the hopper's body, slashing it open.
- Grasshoppers suffer from something called 'summit disease'. It is caused by a fungus. It makes the grasshopper go to the top of a plant, hold the stem tight and die. This way, the fungus makes sure that when it comes out of the dead body, it spreads far and wide. The higher up it is, the more widely it would be carried with the wind. Worldly wise, wouldn't you say?

DANDY DEFENCES

Grasshoppers are not all stupid and aren't always falling prey to other animals. Have you noticed a grasshopper sitting quietly on a leaf, its body slanting, head bent, as if ready

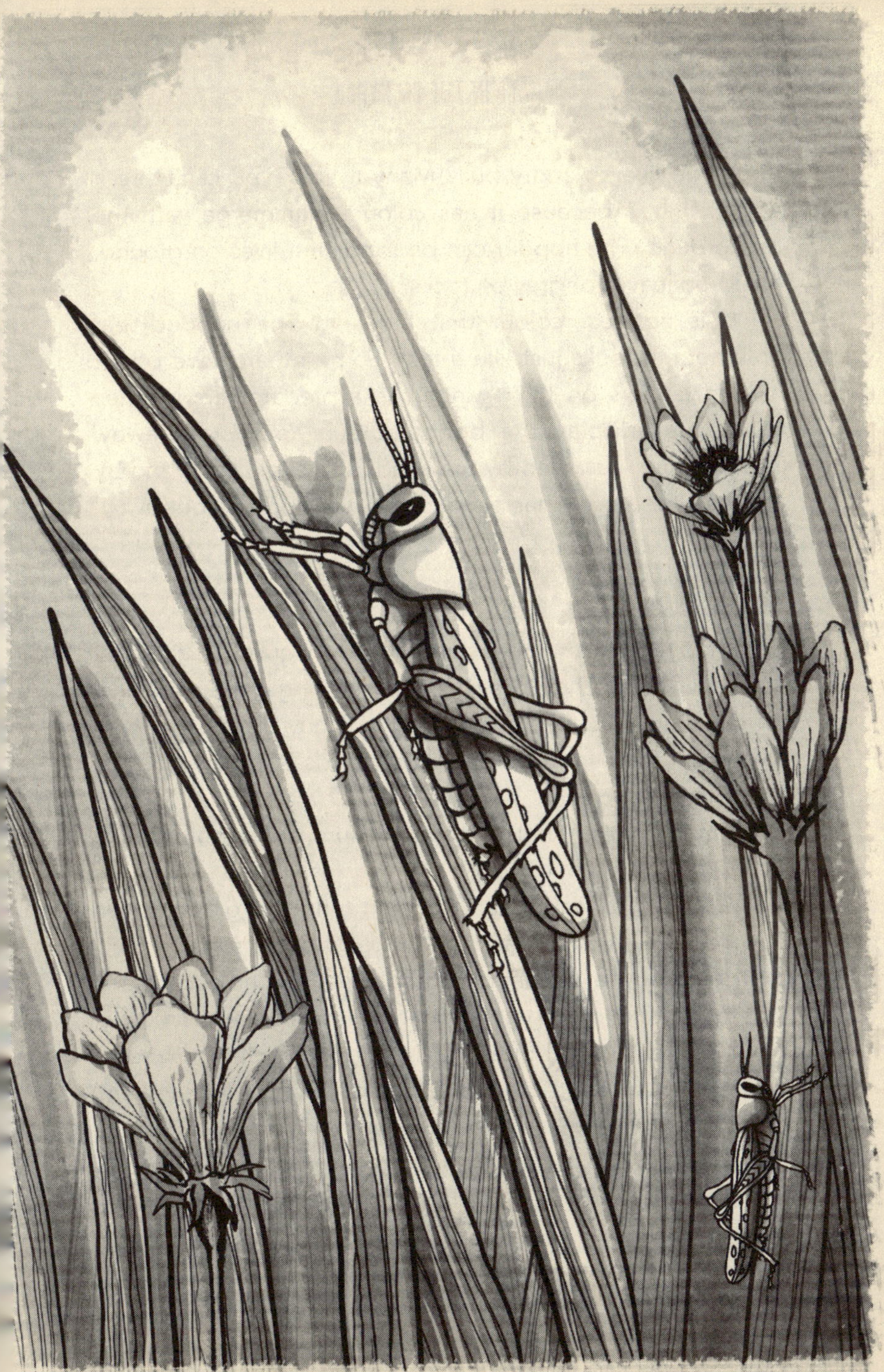

to charge like an angry bull? Many a time, you can't see it at all. That is because it has colours that merge with the background. The hopper can be sandy if it lives on ground, green on leaves or grey on rocks.

It is not just colour that hides it. The hooded leaf grasshopper looks just like a leaf. Some others have bright hidden colours on their wings. As a predator approaches them, they display the bright colours to shoo it away. The predator is startled by the sudden flash of colour and by the time it realizes it has been fooled, the hopper hops away.

HUNGRY HOPPERS

Grasshoppers eat a lot; they specially like our grains, vegetables and other crops. They love sunbathing—lying in the grass and on the leaves. So they live happily in sunny places. The way to prevent them from coming to our fields is to have a lot of shady trees.

Grasshopper: What? No sun, no sunglasses, no coconut water to sip on? I'm off!

We need to watch out for when a normal grasshopper becomes a locust—*that's* when the real trouble starts.

Here's how a shy short-horned grasshopper becomes a lout locust: If a lot of grasshoppers are born in an area, they bump into each other often. This makes them change colour, eat more and breed faster! With their children, grandchildren, great grandchildren and so on, they form large swarms of flying insects. (Imagine—if we bred like that, we'd have to go to school with our children and grandchildren!) These swarms are called plagues. There can be billions of insects in a swarm, and they gorge on all the vegetation of any area they fly by: fruits, bark, stems, seeds, flowers and all.

Be warned, locusts eat *all* vegetables. I hope you are not a couch potato!

There have been swarms of locusts since prehistoric times and they can have horrible effects on human populations. They can finish all our food and cause famines; they can leave an area completely barren. But hey, it's not all bad—their poop leaves the area super fertilized for a bumper crop the following year!

The locust swarms can leave you terrified and open-mouthed. The largest swarm recorded was in 1875, of the Rocky Mountain locusts, which was found in North America. The swarm was around 2900 km long with trillions of insects! The Rocky Mountain locusts are no more, though. It is difficult to imagine that an insect that was found in such large numbers is no longer in existence. The death of this super hopper is still a great mystery scientists are trying to get to the bottom of.

You already know that swarms of locusts are called plagues. Do you know of this other animal that spreads plague? It lives happily in your backyard and shares your food.

RATS! WHO IS THAT?

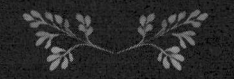

Wherever you live, you're sure to have seen a rat or a mouse. Rounded ears, pointed nose, naked tail (by naked, I mean hairless. Don't go and tell your dad's friend that he has a naked head, now!) and cute whiskers. They live everywhere—cities, villages, towns, jungles, markets, homes, schools, theatres, shopping malls, grain storage houses . . . You name it! What's the difference between a rat and a mouse? They are both rodents; the bigger ones are rats and the smaller ones mice.

RAT RACE

Okay, so let's have a rat race. Complete the given twelve sentences as quickly as possible. The ones to reach the finish line in fourteen minutes will be crowned rat queen or king (Of course, with a score of 12+). Hmm . . . Or maybe it's better that you not be a rat king. You know what that is? Start the rat race to find out!

---

a. tripoding b. bamboo rats c. house mice d. black rats and brown rats e. pee of cats f. the black rats arrived g. a staple diet h. Black Death i. ships j. rat free k. mischief l. a rat king m. brown rats and house mice

---

1. The most popular rats are _____.
2. The most used animals for our researches are _____.

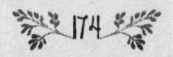

3. In a few parts and cultures of India, Ghana, Hawaii, the Philippines, Thailand, Spain, Cambodia and many other countries, rats are _____.
4. After every forty-eight years in India, some rural areas are invaded by armies of _____.
5. *T. gondii* is the name of a parasite. It makes rats fearless and attracted to _____.
6. Hoppers, crawlies, pinkies, fuzzies and adults are all names of _____.
7. *Rattus rattus* is the name scientists use for the black rats. They spread all over the world by travelling with us in _____.
8. The black rats were one of the main causes of the deadly _____.
9. When a mouse stands up on its hind legs and balances itself with its tail, it is called _____.
10. In Alberta, Canada, they used poison, bombs, poison gas, bulldozers and shotguns when _____.
11. A group of rats is called a _____.
12. A number of rats stuck together by their tails are called _____.

ANSWERS

1. d. black rats and brown rats

Yes. These are the two most well-known of the rats. Both of them are from Asia and have spread all over the world. Rats are some of the deadliest pests and it is quite difficult to have a rat-free area. In the year 1973, there was a huge shortage of food grains in the world. Scientists computed the amount of foodgrains destroyed in India by rats and said that if only we could save these grains, we would overcome the worldwide food shortage! So a rat won't tear you like a tiger or bite you like a banshee *(Banshee: Lies! I don't bite. I just boo.)* but it can leave you hungry. *Very* hungry.

2. m. brown rats and house mice.

Rats spread diseases. But they've saved millions of lives too! How? By helping us discover medicines and increasing our knowledge of surgery. Scientists believe that they share roots with us and have thinking similar to . . . ours! Who else's? We are closely related to them. So brown rats and house mice are used in a lot of experiments. House mice are the more popular subjects for experiments. Scientists have also developed 'knockout rats'. The experiments on these rats help us to understand our diseases and help develop possible cures for them. These rats are a knockout!

3. g. a staple diet

Okay, so rats eat our food. And we eat rats. So many free rats running around in the house . . . good protein diet, right? And they don't even cost as much as chickens and lobsters.

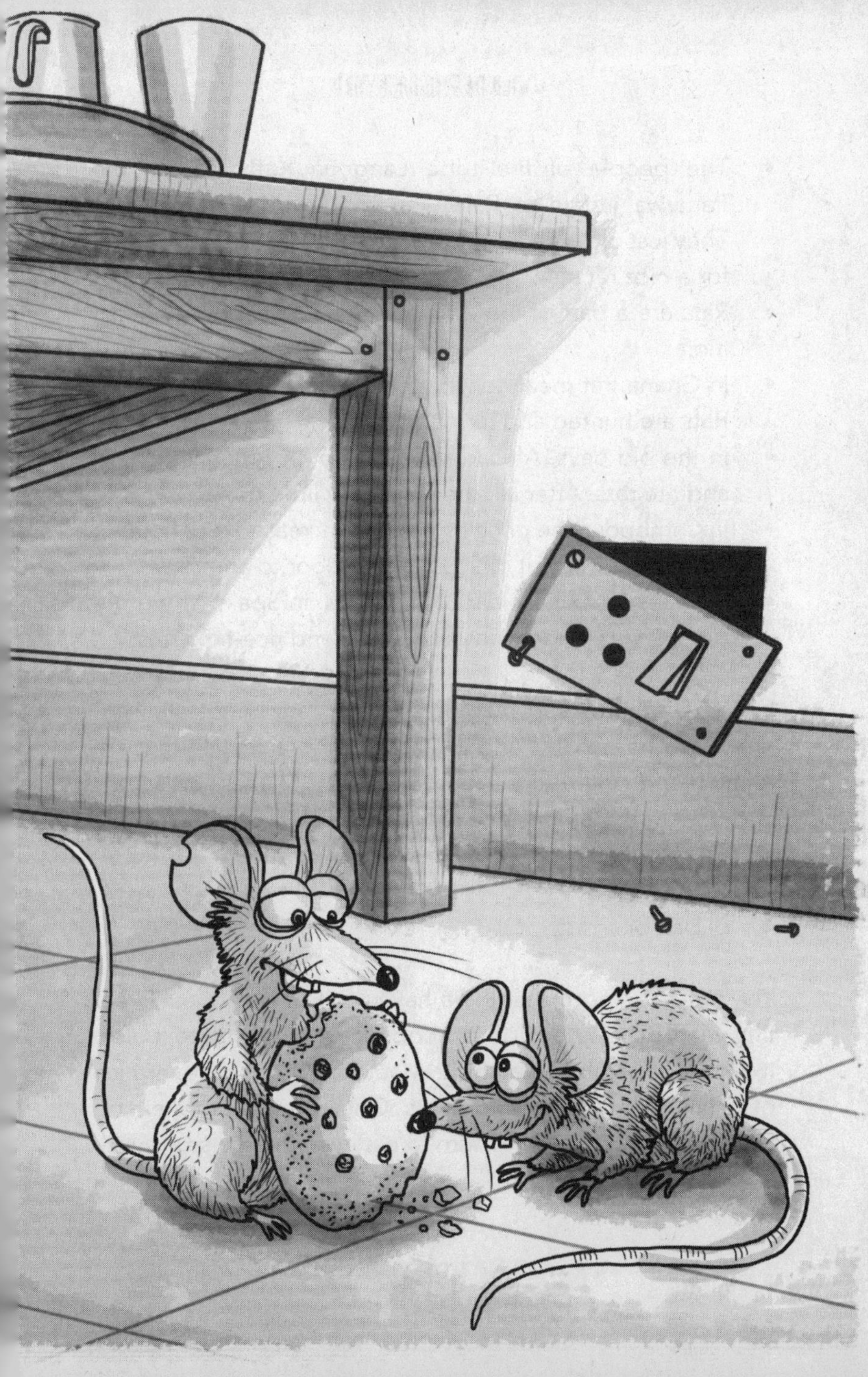

- The people of the tribe Langotia Kathodia—of the Panarwa jungle in Rajasthan—are expert rat-catchers. They just dig up a rathole and take the poor animal home for a nice rat stew.
- Rats are a part of the diet in some cultures of northeast India.
- In Ghana, rat meat constitutes the main part of the diet. Rats are hunted and farmed there.
- In the old days, African slaves in South America hunted and ate rats. After all, they had very little to eat.
- In Cambodia, the price of rat meat increased four times in 2008. That made it difficult for the poor to afford it.
- Paella is an ancient dish of Valencia, in Spain. In the old days, it was made with eels, beans and rice-field rats.

In some cultures and religions, eating rats is not allowed. They say rats are dirty and diseased. Now, animals—that are religion-and-culture-free—gorge on rats. Snakes, owls, cats and a lot of the others love their rat meals.

Rat: Animals, I tell you! No sense of culture!

4. b. bamboo rats

The forests in northeast India have a lot of bamboos. Every fifty years or so, a kind of bamboo blooms just before it dies. It is called 'bamboo death' or *Mautam*. At this time, armies of rats invade villages and fields. Once they're done eating the bamboo flowers, they turn to eat everything else around.

It is called 'rat flood' and can cause terrible food shortage, resulting in many deaths.

The famine caused by rats has even led to revolts! Like the one in Nagaland, for instance. Food shortage caused by rats combined with hardly any help from the government equals the poor, hungry Nagas looting food supplies.

And you thought snakes were the deadliest? Snakes help us in a big way by eating rats. Rats and mice fear cats and owls. But they fear snakes the most as snakes can get inside their burrows at any time.

5. e. pee of cats

Yes, cat's pee. Go figure.

There is a parasite that gets into a rat's head (it is found in humans as well). This parasite is super smart. It delivers its babies in a cat's gut. So how does it get from a rat's body to a cat's gut? It makes the rat's brain foolishly fearless—makes it no longer fear a cat's smell! The rat approaches the cat like a devil-may-care don and when the cat eats the spunky little rat, the parasite happily lays its eggs in the cat's gut.

There's something to think about. Being fearless is not always a great idea—you could end up in a cat's gut.

6. c. house mice

Yes, these Jerries do not have to fear Toms. House mice (not the bigger rats) are kept as pets in many parts of the world.

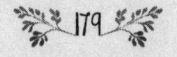

These terms refer to different sizes and ages of the mice sold. House mice are also known to spread diseases, mainly through their poop, but these are not as serious as the ones spread by rats. Anyway, I can't figure why anyone would like to have one more mouse in the house.

7. i. ships

Over thousands of years, we have spread rats all over the world through our voyages. Let's see how:

- Sailors discovered new lands.
- Rats discovered new lands with the sailors. This earned the black rat the name 'ship rat' and the brown rat the name 'wharf rat'.
- Rats killed and ate the local wildlife. (Of course, the settlers also did the same.) Though mice and rats largely eat vegetables, true rats can eat both plants and animals. I think you can guess what happened next.
- Once the rats came into a new area, they multiplied . . . like rats!
- They are the worst pests you can have on an island. The local animals, especially on some islands, had never seen a rat in their lives. They didn't know how to protect themselves and their eggs from these buck-toothed hunters.
- Rats have polished off many kinds of birds, small mammals, reptiles and plants from our planet.

The End. Right?
Wrong.
They continue to do so:

- In south-east Australia, the house mouse lives happily, looking cute. Every three years, its population can reach up to 1000 mice per hectare . . . squeaking plague in your ears!
- There is an island called Gough in the Atlantic Ocean, and it is the only home of the two seabirds, the Tristan albatross and Atlantic petrel. Living on an island with an unlimited supply of fish . . . What else do you need in life, right? But what you don't need are mice. In the nineteenth century, house mice arrived with our ships on Gough Island. Since then, these little mice have grown much, much bigger in size and go about attacking baby birds (which are almost 1 m tall!) in groups. With their cute teeth, they gnaw on them till they bleed to death. And you thought Jerry only ate cheese!

Scientists say that 40–60 per cent of recent seabird and reptile extinctions (animals that have been completely wiped out from the earth, like the dinosaurs) have been caused by rats. Really? Who went to discover and disturb these happy islands and other lands? And who settled there with their pets and pests? Humans. So we are responsible for all the animals becoming extinct. Goodbye moa, goodbye dodo, goodbye elephant bird, goodbye wolves of Falkland . . . Welcome black rats, welcome brown rats, welcome house mice . . .

8. h. Black Death

Between 1346 to 1353, the Black Death happened in Europe. It was one of the most horrible and widespread epidemics in human history. This nasty plague killed 75–200 million people! The Black Death killed 30–60 per cent of Europe's population!

They say this plague was spread by fleas on black rats. The rats' fleas travelled on the rats and the rats travelled on our ships. So actually, this too was spread by humans, don't you think?

9. a. tripoding

A tripod has three legs. The mouse looks like a tripod—balanced on its two hind legs and tail.

Most mice come out at night. They are not only afraid of cats but of rats as well! Rats can kill and munch on mice.

10. f. the black rats arrived

Alberta is the largest area on earth which is free of true rats. How did it manage to remain rat free? Here's how the story goes.

There is no sea in Alberta and so, for hundreds and hundreds of years, rats couldn't hop on to ships and go there. Now, even if they'd somehow managed to get there, the climate in Alberta was not suitable for the rats to survive and thrive. Then finally, in the 1950s, the black rats arrived in Alberta. But as soon as they entered the eastern border, the government started a war against them, and they were hunted down and killed. Guns, bombs, tons of poison, poison gas—they went all out against these invasive rats! The war zone or control area was 600 km long! But see, the use of poison doesn't just keep the rat population in check, it also kills the other animals who eat these poisoned rats.

(A by-story: A similar thing happened in India during the British rule. They also tried to kill rats with poison. But this killed a lot of cats, snakes, owls and other animals who ate the poisoned rats. This further led to an even lower number of rat hunters, and then our rat population exploded—there was nothing to stop them!).

The poison used on rats is also harmful to humans. So the Alberta government stopped attacking with poison. Instead, they used another drug, not as harmful to humans, to kill the rats. 'As harmful,' they say. Maybe it doesn't kill but just leaves us drooling senseless in bed . . . it remains to be seen.

However, even Alberta is not completely rat free. The local pack rats live in the forests there. They are not as nasty as the true rats but they do have a nasty habit: stealing. They love shiny objects—don't we all? And I'm not talking about your dad's shiny bald patch. These pack rats often sneak in and steal jewellery and other such bright, gleaming things from jungle cabins and hotels.

There are other areas, too, where we're at war with rats. (Well, it's better than being at war with each other!) A 'rat team' was sent to the island of South Georgia in 2015.

WILD IN THE BACKYARD

They carried three helicopters and 100 tons of rat poison on a ship! This is to make the island rat free for the seabirds. Let's see who wins the rat war.

11. k. mischief

Yes. Mischief. Quite an apt name.

You know what a male rat is called? A buck. A girl is called a doe. A married lady is called a dam and the babies are called kittens or pups.

12. i. a rat king

Yes. That is what a rat king is—a group of rats stuck by their tails. They are stuck with blood or horse hair or poop or muck or ice—or just knotted. Gross! And they grow together like this. Rat kings have been considered a bad omen by many. Perhaps people feared the very real possibility of them bringing the plague.

There are rat kings in many museums. A museum in Germany even has a mummy of a rat king! It has thirty-two rats tangled by their tails and was found in a miller's fireplace in 1828.

Miller's son: Dad, there is a dead rat king in the fireplace.
Miller: What have I taught you? Grind all titbits with the flour, sonny!

> *Did you know . . .*
>
> Some amount of rat poop is always present in wheat flour! After all, there are so many rats in grain storage areas, it is impossible to not have a teeny-weeny bit in our atta. Unless, of course, you make separate toilets for them and teach them potty manners.

So, you have finished the rat race. Score? Nah, don't worry about it. A rat race is getting to the end without worrying about how you got there. Not a good thing, if you ask me. What, then, would be the difference between you and rats?

WARTIME RATS

Guess who loved World War I? Rats. They ate all the rubbish as well as the soldiers' food in the trenches. Some even came and snatched it away from right under the soldiers' noses! The rats didn't just steal their food but also spread diseases. They grew as fat as cats and bold enough to run over the soldiers while they slept.

Some of the ways the soldiers dealt with these vermin were:

- keeping pet dogs and training them to kill rats
- shooting them

WILD IN THE BACKYARD

- clubing them to death
- battering them with their bare hands (if there was no pot or rock or bayonet in sight)

Enough of the revolting rats. It's time to check out some backyard beauties.

BACKYARD

BEAUTIES

They sing and they dance and they fly and they kill. And we hear them all the time, even if we don't always spot them. Some are dressed in solemn colours like the brothers and sisters in missionary schools. Others, in jazzy blues and pinks and reds and greens—colours you wouldn't be caught dead wearing in public! They fight for their territories. They show off no end to find a mate. They go about their family matters and drop a splash of poop on your head when they feel like it. The birds in our backyards and cities are pretty and smart and savvy. There are many of them, and there are different ones in different regions. Let's check out how a few of these cosmopolitan birds live.

THE TERRIFIC TAILORS

This tailor is not interested in stitching clothes. It is happy with its bright feathers, thank you very much. It uses its tailoring skills to stitch nests. This small warbler—the common tailorbird—is clad in a greenish jacket and a rusty cap. It hops around in the grass and short bushes with its upright tail and sharp beak. You can see it in hedges, dipping its long beak into the necks of flowers to have a nice long sip of nectar. Sometimes, pollen sticks to its head and makes it look as if it had just had its head highlighted in yellow.

The tailorbird is a bug-and-beetle lover. You might see them sometimes, hopping in the grass, looking for one. The tailors prefer to remain hidden in bushes and trees. And you will only know that one is around by its loud calls. Their loud *cheeup-cheeup-cheeup* sounds as though they are carrying a wireless loudspeaker with them.

Neat Nests

The nests of tailorbirds are quite neat. They are not like the ones crows and eagles build. Have you seen a crow's nest? It looks like a broom that got an electric shock! The expert tailor husband and wife dig holes in leaves with their sharp beaks, then, they go steal some spiderwebs or pick up some plant fibre. Using these as thread, they draw it through the leaf holes and neatly tie a knot after each stitch. Once the cradle is ready, they carpet it with soft grass and make it liveable with other suitable furnishings. Mr and Mrs Tailorbird then go about their family affairs and other worldly matters. Not just are they super efficient and hard-working, their long, sticky tongue makes insects go cross-eyed with fear.

There is another bird the insects are dead scared of. From this one, they have no place to hide.

RAT-A-TAT-TAT

Ever seen a woodpecker banging away on a tree trunk? They are a sight, I tell you! Hopping up on a slanting or a straight trunk, stabbing at it like a psycho killer—if you were an insect, that's exactly how you would feel.

The black-rumped flameback is the one that you can spot sometimes in cities and towns. It is one of the most beautiful birds around. It sports golden wings, a sharp beak, a white head and a black throat, and the male goes about like a king, wearing a red crown and crest. The flameback's beak is like a crowbar that digs out hiding insects and worms.

Woodpeckers dip and rise in flight like rough waves. With a rattling call, they hustle around on trees, checking the barks for insects. Their stiff tail provides them with support on the tree trunks as they hammer away at mounds to have their pick of juicy termites. The city-dwelling woodpeckers have an adapted palate and can eat fallen fruits as well as food scraps.

Woodpeckers don't hammer at tree trunks only for a snack. They even dig their nest cavities in them. See, they dig this sort of thing!

Zygodactyl Feet

No, that's not the name of a dinosaur.

Most birds have one toe pointing backward and three facing forward. But the woodpeckers' feet have two toes pointing backward and two forward; this helps them maintain their grip.

If you were banging your head as many times a day as a woodpecker does, you sure would go loony. But there's a reason you don't bang your head against trees and they do! Woodpeckers have neat ways to prevent brain damage. Like:

- short time of contact
- small brain size
- closing of the third eyelid a millisecond before the hit. Yes, some animals have a handy transparent third eyelid for such is the nature of their jobs! It's to protect the eyes from flying pieces of wood.

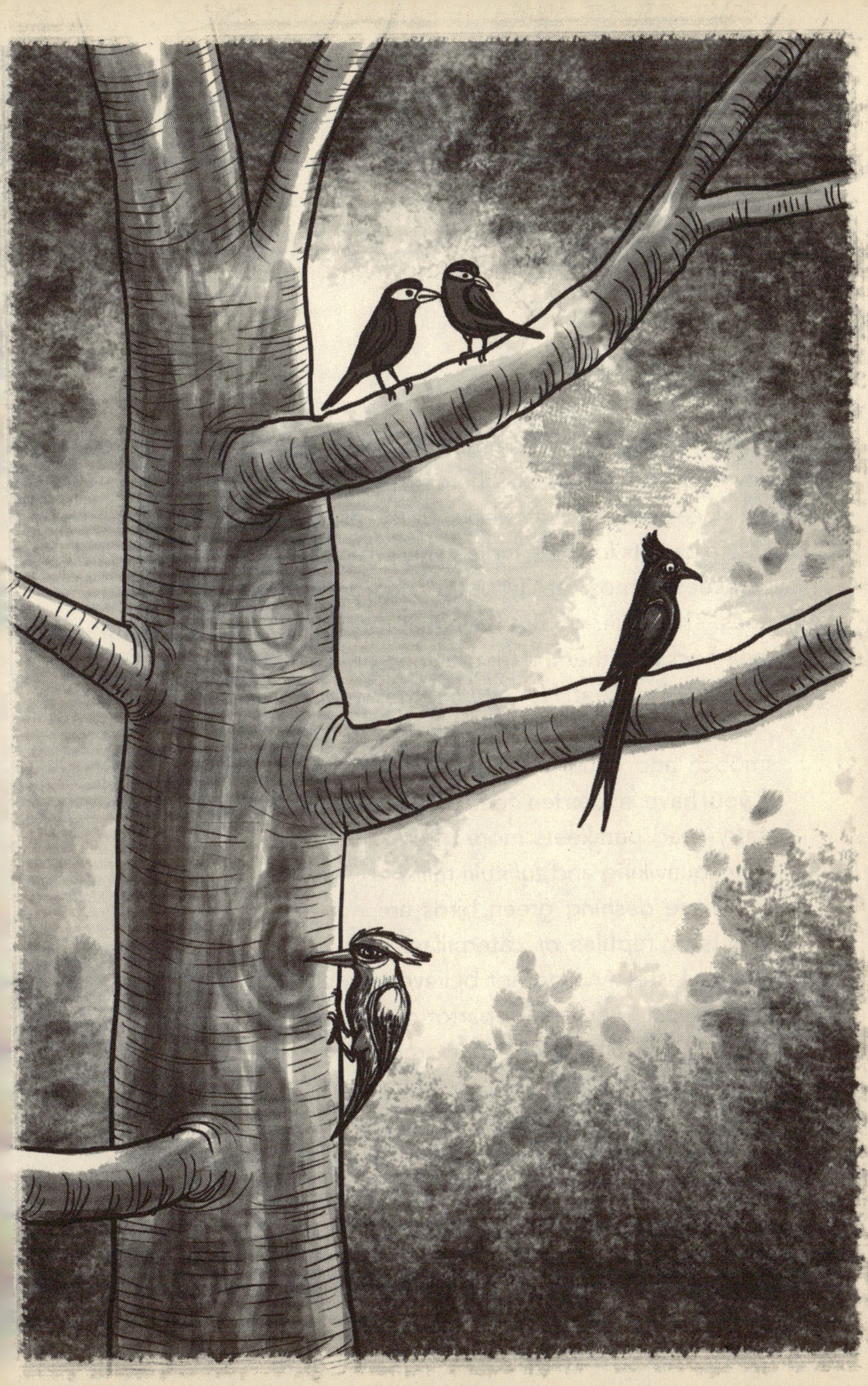

Okay, so these hammering flashy fellows garner a lot of attention. But when this other loud, green bird in love lands on a nearby branch with her boyfriend, you can't help but stare at her.

THE SQUAWKING SMOOCHERS

They may be more common than woodpeckers, but they never fail to interest us—the parrots with their rose-coloured necklaces around their necks. Sorry, did I say parrots? There are no parrots found in India. Only parakeets. The rose-ringed parakeet is most easily seen in gardens that have fruiting trees. The ladies do not have that rose-coloured ring around their necks—either a dark grey one or none at all.

Lady Parakeet: Honey, I'd rather wear a ring on my finger.

When they are in love, there is no stopping them. They smooch and court their beloved like there's no tomorrow. If you have a garden feeder, you will chance upon these starry-eyed parakeets more often. They make a racket with their squawking and *tuiiituiii tuiii*.

These dashing green birds are not at all interested in insects or reptiles or caterpillars. Bah . . . no—they have classier taste! And do not believe in having the whole meal themselves. Ever seen a parrot pick up a berry or fruit with one leg and nibble on it? It drops almost half of the fruit on the ground while nibbling. Other birds and small animals gather on the ground to enjoy the spoils.

Parakeet: That's not wasting, kiddo. That's sharing with the needy.

AREFA TEHSIN

Pleasurable Pets

Parakeets have been kept as pets for ages. The main reason is that they can mimic what we say. 'Hello . . . Howdoyoudo . . . Goodnight . . . *Tuiii* . . . *tuiii*.' And how we love that! We love to see them eat all the green chillies, fruits, nuts and berries we give them.

But we can get real mad at them too—when their wild flocks come and gorge on fruits from our fruit trees and orchards.

Hold on, there is another bird that used to be a popular pet. It is a singer, not a sweet-talker.

THE SINGER IN A TUXEDO

These black-and-white winged opera singers with a straight tail are the magpie robins. Common garden birds, they were caged and kept as pets for their beautiful voices and were also made to participate in bird fights, much like the cockfights of today. Yeah, we don't just fight amongst ourselves—we train our animals to fight as well.

Often active at dusk, they look for insects, geckos, centipedes and leeches, if they can find any. The gents have black bodies, white bellies and a bright white patch on the shoulders. The ladies are greyish-black and white.

The handsome boys go gaga when it is time for them to find a girl. They sing from high branches, puff out their chests, fan their tails and strut about. Maybe you've seen your elder brother act all silly and do something similar in the company of a girl he likes? Except for the fanning-his-tail bit, of course!

This well-dressed bird is not just any other bird in the backyard. No, sir! It is the national bird of Bangladesh!

And though this other bird has no such distinction, it's still pretty cool. It gets a metallic tinge in the sun. Isn't *that* chic?

THE BIRD OF THE SUN

This black-looking bird catches the sunrays on its back and shines a metallic purple. The ritzy-purple sunbird is one of more than hundred kinds of sunbirds found all over our planet. The girls are olive coloured and have delicate, slender bodies. These birds use their long, curved beaks and tube-like tongues to drink nectar from flowers. They hover near these flowers and then perch for a refreshing sip of nectar.

The grown-ups mostly drink nectar but feed their screaming, howling little ones insects in their purse-like nests. What did *you* eat as a baby? Besides what your mum and dad fed you, that is. Chalk and mud, when you could manage it, isn't it?

There is this singing star of a bird, who has the nasty habit of throwing other birds' eggs out of their nests!

THE SLY STAR

The Asian koel is among the most popular birds of India. That is because it can sing . . . like a koel! The sweet rising call of *koo-Ooo, koo-Ooo, koo-Ooo* . . . goes on until it reaches a hysterical pitch. If you have fruit trees, there might be some koels around.

Many great yester-year and current-day female singers are compared to the koel. There are stories and poems praising the beautiful voice of the she-koel. Starry-eyed lovers hear them sing in the rains and let out long sighs. There is only one glitch—the girl is a boy! It is the boy that sings, not the girl! We've made idiots of ourselves with this one!

The koel is a kind of cuckoo, just larger in size. The guy is a glossy, black bird with coal-red eyes. The girl wears a gentle brown robe with white dots on the body and stripes on the tail. And she speaks in a shrill *kik-kik-kik*. The gents usually enter a *koo-Ooo*ing competition to woo the fiery-eyed lady.

Forced Adoption

Here is how this story goes:

Phase I: Once the better guy has impressed the lady, they happily tie the knot. But they don't bother about building a nest. That's what the crows are there for!

Phase II (1): Once they have located a cosy crow home, the daddy koel sings to distract the ma and pa crows. While he's at it, the mummy koel quietly goes and lays her eggs in the crow's nest.

Phase II (2): More often than not, the daddy koel is good-for-nothing and leaves it to the mummy koel to slyly approach the crow's nest alone. If need be, she tosses away one of the crow's eggs to make space for her own. How convenient.

WILD IN THE BACKYARD

Phase III: The crow parents are invariably fooled. The koel chicks generally hatch before the crow chicks and feast on all the goodies brought in by their foster parents. And the crow couple never realizes what's going on. At times, the mummy koel decides to visit the nest (when the crow couple is not around, of course) and brings a small snack—a lizard or a caterpillar—along for the shouting babies she left behind.

Phase IV: Once the chicks grow up, they prefer to eat fruits. And then they go about looking for girlfriends and boyfriends—and, of course, other crow households to lay their eggs in.

The other black bird in our backyards can't fool the crafty crow like the koel can, but it is daring and bad tempered. No wonder it is called the king crow.

THE BIRD WITH A FORK

No, it doesn't use a fork to eat—it has a forked tail. The black drongo is a hotheaded black bird. If you have open areas around your backyard, it might pay you a visit. You can see it perched upright on a telephone line or a bare branch, gazing into nothing. But don't be fooled—that is its hunting strategy! As soon as an insect flies by, lost in its insect-dreams, the drongo launches its attack.

Worker Bee: You wouldn't believe it, Queen. Beethoven was flying right behind my bum. And then, just with a gust of wind, he was gone!

Queen Bee: You sure you didn't fart?

The black drongos also visit fields that are being ploughed. They love themselves a little beetle grub or some caterpillars upturned with the soil.

Hotheaded Loony

Oh yes, these fellows are fearless. If Mr and Mrs Drongo have built a nest on a tree, they protect it like loonies. They just dive-bomb any large birds of prey that even *try* to dilly-dally near their tree. Other small birds like bulbuls, orioles, pigeons and babblers try to build their nests in the same tree. Because then they don't have to worry about freeloaders trying to eat their eggs and chicks, what with the hotheaded drongos around to shoo them away.

The Con-bird

There are more than twenty-five different kinds of drongos. Most of them are black and some of them are great tricksters. So what's the trick?

- Drongos generally give a warning call when there is a hunter around. Many animals and birds hear their call and take off. The common drongo of the Kalahari Desert in Africa, however, has a better plan. Sometimes, even when there is no hunter around, this drongo calls in warning. When the birds and animals have fled, it feasts on all the delicious beetles and bugs by itself. It can even mimic the warning calls of meerkats, sending them to

their hiding places, and then it proceeds to eat their food as well!
Meerkat 1: Now who's the clown who called in the warning?
Meerkat 2: Boss, this wise guy here—Surricat—did it.
Meerkat 3: I did not!
Meerkat 2: You did too!
Meerkat 3: Did not!

- The greater racket-tailed drongo talks in a sharp *tunk-tunk-tunk*. But it has this unusual, clever habit. It mimics the voices of other birds and animals. Shikra is a bird of prey which gives all the birds the jitters. The minute one is seen or heard on a nearby tree, all the birds scat as soon as, and wherever, possible. The clever drongo imitates the shikra's call to scare away the birds and steal their food.
Drongo: Ah . . . nothing like a quiet, six-course dinner.

The greater racket-tailed drongo can imitate even the voice of the seven sisters (who are not sisters anyway).

THE SEVEN SISTERS

These birds, with their drab brown clothes and yellow eyes, you wouldn't care to look at them twice, are called the seven sisters. They aren't always seven or actual sisters. But they do babble away—*kay-kay-kay-kay*.

They are the jungle babblers. They roam in groups of six or seven, or sometimes more, and are called 'saath bhai' in Hindi. That means seven brothers. Don't ask me who translated their name! This sisterhood or brotherhood or sister-brother-hood of travelling birds skulks in the bushes and the undergrowth in our gardens, as well as in jungles.

Always with an angry frown on their faces, they go about fluffing, puffing and eating together. And grooming each other with their beaks if need be. The boss generally flies from a branch first, followed by the stumbling group. They go around digging into piles of fallen leaves, looking for insects. A random meal of berries and nectar is also welcome, though!

There is generally one top pair that breeds in a season, and everyone in the gang looks after the chicks—all for one and one for all! They create one big racket wherever they are (which is generally our gardens).

There is another bird in your garden, who might not scowl like the babblers, but goes around wearing a bandit mask, and sometimes, even behaves like one.

THE MASKED BANDIT

With a brown body, a black hooded head, yellow legs and bill, and a bright yellow patch around the eyes, the common mynah is one of the most common birds seen in our gardens. It has taken very well to city lifestyle. Although it may look totally composed when it moves around, this one's a real hothead! In Sanskrit, it is called *kalahapriya*, which means 'one who is fond of arguments'.

Can you tell if the statements below are true?

1. The common mynah can speak in a human voice.
2. It prefers to live alone.

WILD IN THE BACKYARD

3. It can use snakeskin to build its nest.
4. In Australia, they call it the flying rat.
5. It flaps its wings while singing.

ANSWERS

1. true

It can mimic the human voice. The hill mynah is a master of mimicry. Much better than your 'Ram-Ram'-saying parakeet. That is why they were once quite popular as pets.

The common mynah squawks and chirps and whistles and croaks and even growls! Or just shouts a warning to warn its mate and other friends if there is a hunter in the area. Before it goes to sleep, it joins its call with other mynahs. Maybe they sing themselves a goodnight song. Or just wish each other goodnight.

Mynah 1: Nighty-night!
Mynah 2: Sweet dreams!
Mynah 1: Sleep tight!
Mynah 3: If you're going to snore like a machine gun, sleep on another branch!

2. false

Mynahs generally live in pairs. If you see one in your garden or on your windowsill, there will be another one around.

Some people believe that mynahs have just one sweetheart for life. Mynahs, with their sweethearts, have spread to many parts of the world from Asia.

3. true

Shed snakeskin, twigs, roots, rubbish, tissue paper, tin foil—they can use all of these to line their nests. They nest in the hollows of trees. Most of the time, they use the ready-made nests of other birds like woodpeckers. And they don't shy away from having fierce battles with other birds—they chase them away from their nests and even jab and wrestle if need be. Their ready-to-fight attitude has led them to occupy new regions easily. Don't they sound like a few of our countries?

But the clever koel beats the mynah here. Like it does with the crow, it sneaks in and lays its eggs in a mynah's nest—super cons to fool the bandits!

4. true

There are so many of them in Australia! And they don't just fight with other birds—you can also see them hopping alongside the cattle in the fields, catching and eating insects and grasshoppers disturbed by their grazing. It's not just other birds and cattle they mooch from, they also like to eat the Australians' food and grains.

They eat lizards and insects and fruits and grains, and even look for stray scraps in garbage bins. If nothing else, they'll just go and eat a baby sparrow or steal from your dog's plate. But they have a particular liking for grasshoppers. That is why they are also called grasshopper hunters.

5. false

They bob their heads while singing. And fluff their feathers as well. These bandits are fun to look at when they walk around in our gardens or ledges. They are not only a pleasure to watch, they have a sweet, soothing voice when they sing too.

Now, there is another bird that outnumbers this moody bandit in our cities. You will find it sitting on statues and pooping—I mean, painting—them white.

THE MESSENGERS

A loud clap or bang, and their flock will fly away, circle the sky and then settle again. The blue rock pigeon is a bird that can be easily shooed away. Bluish-grey birds with two dark grey wing bands, rock pigeons are seen in city squares, parks and streets, pecking or sitting in flocks. They either feed on birdseed given by pigeon lovers or on leftover grains. They look gently at you but they are big show-offs too. By puffing out their bodies, the boys move round and round in circles. When they're in love, they smooch away on your window, not caring if you're watching them goggle-eyed. There was a time when they were found only in the wild but now, they are as much city residents as we are, almost all over the world.

Don't underrate these regular-looking birds next door. Not just *any* bird can live happily in the big bad human cities.

AREFA TEHSIN

THE ROCK STARS

Can you spot the wrong one in the following ten rocking pigeon facts?

1. The first pigeon was tamed 10,000 years ago.
2. Rock pigeons are among the favourite foods of hawks, eagles, owls and humans.
3. Train a domestic pigeon. Release it a thousand kilometres away. It will find its way back home.
4. The pigeon Cher Ami was a wartime heroine. She saved the lives of many American soldiers.
5. A flying group of pigeons is called a kit.
6. Pigeon fanciers are those who raise domestic pigeons.
7. Pigeons can live more than three times their lives when bred in captivity (in a cage or zoo or bird park).
8. They look V-shaped while gliding.
9. Blue rock pigeons were brought into the US and Canada by settlers who came from Europe.
10. White pigeons are released on birthdays.

ANSWER

All except the last statement are correct.

1. That's what the scientists think. They say it's the world's oldest bird to be tamed! We didn't tame them to just make pets of them and give them bucketfuls of grain to

eat. Pigeons are also bred to be fed to other pets. Why, did you think you could only breed chickens for yourself?

2. Pigeons are peaceful birds. So they just fly away to escape predators. If they can't take off in time, hard luck! Cats love to munch on pigeon meat. The birds of prey who live in cities, like owls, hawks, eagles and even jungle crows, love their pigeon pie. They see them sitting together on a building or an electricity pole and dive down to attack. A hawk or eagle may fly away with one. A crow may just catch hold of another by its wing or neck. It may then jab at it till it dies. A hundred other pigeons around may just watch the spectacle and not come to help. They are peaceful birds, after all.

Oh, did I forget to tell you this? Humans breed pigeons to eat them too. The baby pigeons gather a lot of baby fat before they can fly. They are called squabs. Now, some of us love to eat squabs. We've bred and developed a special king pigeon so we can eat its squabs. Remember the witch who fed Hansel and Gretel to make them chubby before she ate them? I think we learnt the trick from her.

3. The pigeons have a strong homing instinct. That means, if you take them to a totally new place and leave them there (again, like Hansel and Gretel), they will find their way back home. And without the trail of pebbles or breadcrumbs, mind you! Domestic pigeons are trained to become homing experts. And they can travel a thousand kilometres from unknown lands back home!

4. Many trained pigeons are wartime heroines and heroes. What's more, they have even been given medals

for bravery! They've carried crucial messages on time from one place to another and saved many human lives. There are thirty-two pigeons who've received bravery awards in World War II. G.I. Joe (no, not the muscled fighting men!) from America and Paddy from Ireland are two among them.

5. Yes, they are. I don't get why they call them a kit. But the pigeons can certainly do with a kit to make their nests, which are untidy and loose. The nests are made of leaves and twigs, which are later stuck together by the baby pigeons' poop.

6. Seen a white or brown or spotted or pale or rusty pigeon among the others? Pigeon fanciers breed fancy pigeons of different shapes, sizes and colours. Some pigeons escape and go out to live in our crazy, wild cities. How do the fanciers breed them as they please? By selective breeding, of course.

    Pigeon fancier: Jagmohan, you are an obedient boy. You always return home on time. You must marry Flapper, the high-flyer. Your child, Jagflapper, will fly fast and return home on time.

    Well, selective pairing is not done by pigeon fanciers alone; many parents and uncles and aunts also love to do the same—with their children, who else?

    Aunt: You know who'll be the perfect boy for our Paro? Arre . . . Harikishan from Chirmiri!

7. Generally, rock pigeons live up to five years in the wild. They can go on living up to fifteen years or more in a nice cosy cage!

8. They hold their wings in a tight V shape as they glide, when they are tired of flying. What do you do when you're tired of walking? Sit. Common sense!
9. Rock pigeons were only found in some parts of Asia, Africa and Europe. The Europeans brought them along to North America in the 1600s. Just as pets. Not to carry their love letters back to Europe. That was more than a thousand kilometres away. *Way* more.

The Passengers of the Past

We talked about the messengers. Now let's talk about the passengers. Unlike the rock pigeons, the passenger pigeons are no more. Found in North America, passenger pigeons were, at one point, the most abundant birds in the world! There were 3–4 billions of them! Days turned into nights when their flocks passed by. Once, in 1813, the birder John James Audubon was travelling in his wagon from the Ohio River. A flock of passenger pigeons passed over him, blocking the afternoon sun. When he reached Louisville at sunset, the flock was still passing overhead. For the next three days, other flocks followed the first one. He calculated that a flock one mile wide, passing for three hours a mile per minute, would consist of around 1,01,50,36,000 birds! And this was just a fraction of their population! What happened to them, you ask? We ate them and shot them for sport, all the billions of passengers. In the year 1914, the last of the passenger pigeons died. Today, not a single passenger bird is alive. Really, we *do* beat the rats at it. Big time.

10. Now this one's incorrect. It is a custom to release white pigeons at funerals and weddings. No, not at birthday parties. Pity, isn't it? Where do they get the white pigeons to release? From companies who breed and train homing pigeons through selective breeding. You can feel all sappy, red-eyed and runny-nosed when a white pigeon flies away to freedom, but actually, these fancy pigeons just return home to the company that owns them. Fancy *that*! The homing pigeons are also used for pigeon racing. Yes, it is a sport. They are also used for carrying messages and love letters between people.

So we've talked about a few of our backyard beauties. Let's now check out some real slimy and sluggish stuff crawling around in our porches and gardens.

THE SLIMY AND THE SLUGGISH

They are slimy. They are sluggish. They leave a long, shiny path behind them as they walk. They carry their homes on their backs. And their hearts on their legs (not on their sleeves as they don't have any hands). Only one long, *long* leg. You don't have to think at snail's pace to know what I am talking about!

Snails are found on land, in the sea and in ponds and lakes, deserts and ditches. And of course, in our backyards. If you so much as touch them, they squeeze themselves inside their shells. Just like tortoises. They like to come out on our porches and gardens in the rains—nothing like a shower during an evening walk.

WHO'S WHO?

There are thousands of different kinds of snails but the ones we generally see are land snails. Most snails live in the depths of the seas and there are many who live in fresh water. Scientists are still scratching their heads, trying to find out how many! The water snails have gills and the land snails have lungs. Wait a minute, that's not correct—some land snails have gills and some water snails, lungs! Well, who's who then?

It's just that snails love wet homes. Even when they live on land, they like to hang around wet, muddy places. Don't you too? They are more or less amphibious.

Once you find the good eggs from each of these fact baskets, you'll be a super snail expert.

1. Most snails have (thousands/ hundreds/ dozens) of teeth.
2. Slugs are snails without (teeth/ shell/ attitude).

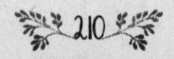

3. Snail shells are good for (wrinkles/ toothache/ the tongue twister, 'She sells seashells on the seashore.')
4. Snails are (soft/ chewy/ slimy) to eat.
5. Land snails use (sweat/ mucus/ saliva) to crawl.
6. Visitors eat (12/ 1/ 5) tons of snails during the three-day Snail Festival in Spain.
7. Most of the land snails are (ladies/ gents/ both ladies and gents at the same time).
8. 'Snail mail' means (email/ postal mail/ a male snail).
9. Most land snails have eyes on their (tentacles/ shells/ muscular legs).
10. A flatworm called the green-banded broodsac can take a particular marsh snail (on a suicide mission/ to a party/ to a swimming pool).

THE GOOD EGGS

1. thousands

Yes, thousands of teeth! Imagine how happy a snail dentist would be. These tiny teeth are located on their tongue, which is called a radula. The ribbon-like tongue shreds their food into tiny scraps. Most land snails eat vegetarian food—algae, fungi, leaves, stems, fruits, leaves . . . That is why some of them are pests in fields. But there are kids who keep garden snails as pets. They like to see the snails' slimy trails as they crawl ahead, and they feed them veggies and fruits along the way.

2. shell

Slugs are snails without shells. There are also snails with shells *so* small that they can't hide inside them. Want to try guessing what they are called? Semi-slugs! Slugs can hide from their hunters better than snails. Without the shell, they can just squeeze beneath a log or stone. Squ-easy! Get it?

3. wrinkles

And for saying, 'She sells seashells on the seashore' too! Yes, there are some kinds of snails that are used as make-up ingredients as well—they help get rid of aches and scars and wrinkles.

Snail: Kill me for wrinkles? Who's that?

4. chewy

How do I know that? Because the French say so. And the Filipinos and the Spanish and Vietnamese and Cambodians and Nepalese and Chinese and Algerians and Indians and . . . Snails are eaten almost all over the world, and have been for thousands of years.

- *Sate Kakul* is an Indonesian fried snail satay.
- Escargot is one of the French and Spanish snail dishes.
- Eggs of some kinds of snails are eaten like caviar.

Did you know that breeding snails to eat them is called heliciculture? And it must be—for them.

Snail: What the hell-is-this-culture, man!

The largest land snail is the giant African snail, which can weigh up to 1 kg! The largest sea snail is the false trumpet—it can weigh up to 18 kg! What is *your* weight, by the way?

5. mucus

If you have seen a snail crawl, you would also have seen a shiny path left behind it. This is the mucus snails release to crawl smoothly. They have a muscular leg, which moves like a wave and glides over the mucus. They like to live in wet homes, remember? The mucus helps their bodies not to dry up. You might find these little critters soft and slimy. But you know what? A soft snail can actually crawl over the edge of a razor without getting a cut!

Your dad: Not get cut by a razor?! I wish I had mucus on my cheeks. (eww!)

6. 12 tons

It is a hit festival visited by a lot of snail-hungry fellas.

In Greece, you can even buy a live snail at a few supermarkets!

7. both a lady and a gent at the same time!

Most of the land snails are 'hermaphrodites'. This fancy word means they are both a he and a she. Depending on whom they meet for the evening, they decide what they're going to be.
Snail 1: Hello there, lady.
Snail 2: Snotty Snail-pace from Grade 3! I am not a girl, boy!
Land snails lay their eggs in clutches in the soil.

8. postal mail

You guessed it right! Because it is slow. It's nothing close to an SMS or an email. But letters sent by post have their own charm and mystery, wouldn't you agree?

9. tentacles

They are also called eyestalks. Though snails can hardly see, for what it's worth, they do still have eyes and they're located on their tentacles.
The life span of a snail varies in different kinds of snails. However, if they are kept properly and taken care of in a cage or zoo (captivity, remember?), they live much longer. Some kinds of snails can even live up to fifteen years in captivity—maybe more!

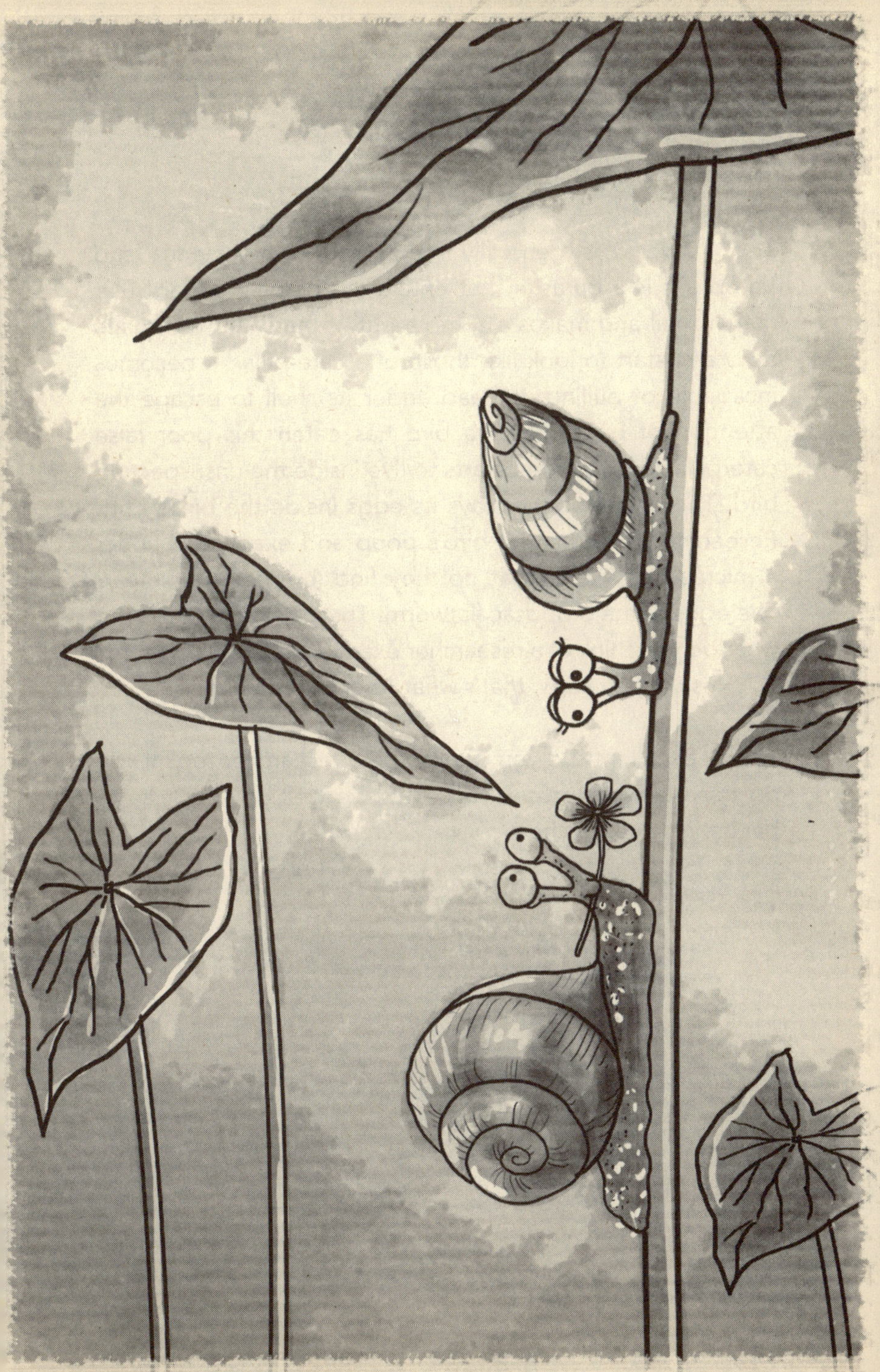

10. on a suicide mission

This flatworm is generally found in North America and Europe. It is a parasite that enters the body of a particular marsh snail and makes a zombie out of the snail. The snail's eyestalks start to look like those of a caterpillar. It becomes incapable of pulling its head under its shell to escape the attention of birds. Once a bird has eaten this poor false caterpillar, the flatworm starts to live inside the unsuspecting bird. The broodsac then lays its eggs inside the bird's butt. Researchers pick up the bird's poop and examine it under a microscope—and what do they find (besides the smell)? The eggs of the broodsac flatworm! That's gross, isn't it? And what do you think of a researcher examining a bird's bottom?

Researcher: Now, that's what I call bottoms up!

Ah . . . Excellent! Do you want to be a researcher too? If you do this backyard probe, you could be well on your way to becoming a researcher!

THE BACKYARD PROBE

Twinkle, twinkle little star,
An owl is sitting not too far,
A bat is flying in the sky,
A bedbug's crawling up my thigh . . .

See, there are so many animals in your backyards, gardens and homes, living with you. A dragonfly whirring its wings like a helicopter. Or a blister beetle ready to give you a blister in the rains. Or a colony of termites eating away into your wooden door.

The dragonflies and damselflies eat away the killer mosquitoes, while bulbuls pick and eat the insects who give you the creeps. The housefly doesn't scare you out of your pants. You'd wave your hand if it sat on your face and say, 'Fly away, fly!' Well, as it sits grinning and rubbing its hands in delight over your food, it may just be spreading a disease that can leave your dribbling. Where did you think it sat before it came buzzing to your cake? In a drain or on your poodle's poop, most likely.

Some of the critters are awake with us in the day. Others wake up when we go to bed. Many of them have much more interesting lives than we do—turning into zombies, nocturnal hunting, tearing flesh with their teeth and claws, flying sky-high, diving down like missiles, dancing and singing, having gang wars and fights, climbing up walls like Spider-Man, no homework and no worrying about what to wear . . .

AREFA TEHSIN

Let's see if you can match the descriptions below to the critters that frequent your backyard.

A PROBE IN THE BACKYARD

1. You don't eat us. You don't eat our eggs. You eat our food. Those of us you see are our women most of the time. They're quite hard working, really. And only the ladies sting! The gents are just sweet-talkers.
2. I live in your bed and I am active at night when you go to sleep. I've fed on human blood for thousands of years. I just drink a teeny-weeny bit of your blood and give you a small rash. Now, that's not too much for keeping a little critter alive, is it?
3. I look like a snake but I'm not one. I live on the ground, dig burrows and my 1500 different kinds of relatives are found almost all over the world. If you're calling me over for dinner, make sure there are lots of insects, snails, slugs, millipedes and earthworms. You could keep some fruits and salads as starters. Oh, and even if you serve me my own tail on a platter, I won't mind.
4. I like to live in your cupboards, bathrooms, kitchens, attics and other such dark, humid places. The night is the time to party, isn't it? So I come out at night—I'm not too fond of the light, since you ask. I like to nibble on glue, cloth, photos, sweets, coffee and even your dandruff. I can even have my own shed skin for dinner if I decide, you know. Not too fussy like that!

5. We are big social wasps who like our diet of nectar and rotten sweet fruits. But don't think we're sugar-sweet. We can attack in a swarm. And we sting much harder than honeybees!
6. I am a great jumper. Is that the reason you like to eat my legs? I lay my eggs in water. My kids have tails and gills, but I am tailless. I breathe through my skin. Even *drink* through my skin, by the way. You can see me in your garden, mostly during the rains. I fill air in my vocal sacs and call out to my sweetheart. The 4800 of our different kinds do not just croak. We all actually have our own languages. We *ribbit*, *jug o' rum*, *brekekekex-koax-koax*, *plop-plop-plop* and speak in several other tongues.
7. I look like a butterfly, but I'm only its cousin. Bats, owls, lizards and other such freeloaders like to eat... you know who—Moi! I am really clever too. Many of my relatives can mimic other creatures like hornets, tarantulas and praying mantises. Now those sting and bite, don't they? They aren't peaceful like me. I can always pretend to be them to avoid the freeloaders. One of my kinds even mimics bird poop. No one would want to eat *that*! I generally come out at night and like to dance wild around your lights. You aren't the only one who knows how to party!
8. You know what Charles Darwin, your great naturalist, wrote about me? He said he doubts if many other animals have played so important a part, as I have, in the history of the world!

   Need I say more?

AREFA TEHSIN

> a. frog/toad b. earthworm c. honeybee d. skink e. silverfish
> f. bedbug g. hornet h. moth

ANSWERS

1. c. honeybee

Honeybees are social insects, like ants. They have provided us with honey and beeswax for a long, long time. We get our honey from beekeepers. Some of it is also collected from the wild.

Here are a few burly bee facts.

- One queen rules the colony. She is top class. Her only job is to lay eggs. And isn't she good at it! She can lay up to 2000 eggs a day! A colony of honeybees can have tens of thousands of worker bees (up to 60,000!), who are all ladies. They come second to the queen. And then there are a few thousand drones (gents), but they don't have a sting. As in the case of ants, their only job is to woo the queen.
  Worker bee to drone: You're third class, honey.
- The worker bees clean the hive, feed the queen's brood (their brothers and sisters), gather nectar from flowers, guard the hive and circulate air by beating their wings. A few are assigned the duty of an undertaker—they take the dead bees out of the hive. The bees that we usually see are all ladies.
  Drone to us: No wonder you get stung.
- The drones are kicked out of the hive in winter. The bees huddle up around the queen to keep warm, and they live

on stored honey and pollen. The larvae are given 'royal jelly' to start with—honeybees secrete this protein-rich jelly to feed to the larvae—after which they're fed pollen. By spring, the hive has a new generation of bees.

- If a queen dies, the workers can turn a normal larva into a queen by continuing to feed her the 'royal jelly'!
- If you disturb their hive, they can launch an attack—an all-women's army like the Amazons!
- Bees are becoming rarer and rarer in the wild. How many flowers and jungles do we have left anyway? We've cut down jungles and built our cities everywhere. But if you have a lot of fruiting trees and flowers in your area, you might have a beehive in your own backyard!

Did you know . . .

Scientists say that if there were no more bees left in the world, the human race would not survive!

- Have you seen a fat bumblebee hovering above the flowers in your garden? They're the closest relatives of honeybees.

2. f. bedbug

Have your mum and dad ever said, 'Good night, sleep tight. Don't let the bedbugs bite'? Bedbugs, which were more common before the 1950s, still live on many of our beds.

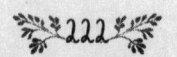

They are light brown bloodsucking insects. The colour of these little flat insects (just 4–5 mm long) changes to bright red for some time right after they've had a filling meal. Oh, and they smell when they are crushed. Centipedes, cockroaches and other such slightly bigger bullies eat bedbugs.

During World War II, the American soldiers had to fight these bugs as well. It doesn't require much effort to guess who the winner was—yes, the bedbugs! Countries like the US now have bedbug-detection dogs! They are taken to people's homes to detect these bugs.

Dog 1: Why are you pulling a face? Do you smell a bedbug?
Dog 2: Yuck! It's the boy's socks!

3. d. skink

Skinks are lizards with long tails and short limbs. Some have no limbs and hardly any neck. That's what makes them look like snakes. Generally, they chill beneath the mud, in burrows, safe from hunters. They can shed their tail like the house gecko when under attack. Some skinks, like the five-lined and slender skinks, return to eat their shed-off tails later. They seem to have taken their ma and pa's lesson, 'Don't let anything go to waste!' too seriously.

4. e. silverfish

The silverfish, a small insect without wings, is one of the oldest insects in the world.

And, as the name suggests, it is silver in colour and moves and looks like a tiny fish. It can live for two to even eight years. If you've ever tried to squash one, you'd know that they're great runners. That's how they escape the centipedes and spiders who come looking for a mock-fish meal.

Silverfish: Who are you calling 'old', buddy? I am two and kicking!

5. g. hornet

Hornets, the hotheaded wasps, are social insects, like honeybees. The nests housing their colonies are built in the open on trees and bushes. A few may build nests in cavities. (If you've plucked a fruit which a hornet is digging into, all the best!) They kill a lot of insects, including honeybees and grasshoppers. They mash these protein-rich insects and feed them to their hungry little larvae. Once they grow up, they generally just eat nectar and other sweet things.

You might see one if there are fruiting trees in your garden. One of the most common hornets in India is the banded hornet.

Deadly Detail

Honeybees die after they sting you. Why? Because their barbed sting is dragged out of their body and remains stuck in your skin. But hornets don't have barbed stings. They can sting you as many times as they like. And live happily ever after!

6. a. frog/toad

The wide-eyed frogs, who look at the world with wonder, are amphibians. They are carnivores. And some of them call so loud that you can hear them a mile away! The frogs that have warts on their skin are called toads. That isn't very nice—how would you like it if someone called you 'homo-wartus' because of your pimples?

Frogs come in various colours and many of them are experts at camouflage. Some can look just like the rock they live upon—others, like the leaf of a tree. Oh yes, there are tree frogs too. The Asian tree frog builds a nest of froth on a branch right above the water. As soon as the tadpoles (baby frogs) hatch, they fall directly into the water. And the ma and pa are free to go sing on another tree.

Freaky Frog Fact

Frog legs are eaten in a lot of countries. The population of frogs has gone down a lot. They say that since the 1980s, more than 120 kinds of frogs have become extinct. This is not only because we eat their legs but also because of the increasingly polluted air and water. Remember frogs breathe and drink through their skin?

In Rajasthan, millions of frogs were caught and their legs exported. Since frogs eat mosquitoes, fewer frogs means more mosquitoes. Naturalist Dr Raza Tehsin fought to stop the export of frogs. And after much protest, it was banned by the government of Rajasthan. Not Raza's protest, the export of frogs!

Frog to princess: Eww . . . Don't kiss me! I don't want to become your prince . . . You'll eat away my legs!

7. h. moth

A moth is an insect most often confused with a butterfly. But it comes out at night and sits with both its wings always spread.

Did you know . . .

The silkworm is the caterpillar of the silk moth! We farm it for its silk, which it uses to build its cocoon.

Death's Head

There are lots of other interesting kinds of moths. One has a skull-shaped design on its back. It is called the death's-head hawkmoth. It has starred in Bram Stoker's *Dracula* and the movie *The Silence of the Lambs*. This moth doesn't just have a skull on its back, it has a nasty squeak when it is irritated.

Animals routinely figure in our art and culture, movies and cartoons. And, of course, our languages. Do you squeak or roar, hiss or yelp, growl or snarl, bark or yap or howl when you're angry?

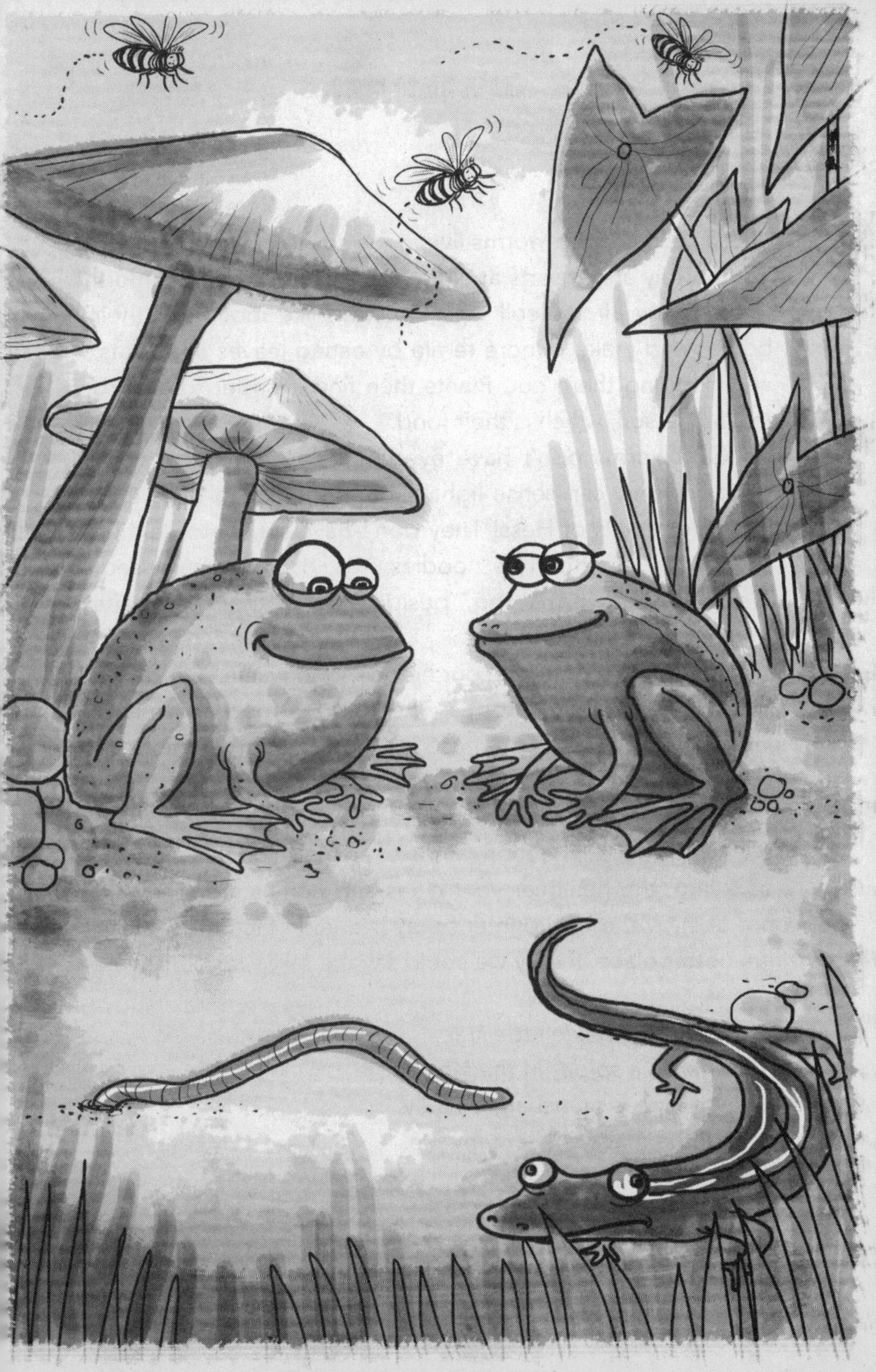

8. b. Earthworm

These tube-shaped worms live in the soil in our gardens and fields. They are experts at airing the soil and making it more fertile. They air the soil with the wave-like motion of their bodies and make it more fertile by eating leaves and roots, and pooping them out. Plants then find it easier to absorb this fertile soil, which is their food.

Earthworms don't have eyes but they have a positive outlook—they can sense light through these cool cells they have, light cells of Hess! They don't have a skeleton either, so humans eat them as noodles. Yes, don't be surprised. We eat earthworms too, besides using them as baits for fishing.

A nice way to recycle our home's food waste is to dump it in a pit full of earthworms. They eat the food and turn it into fertilizer. We can then use it to fertilize our flower beds and gardens.

There are many other little and big critters who share our living space. The more kinds of animals you have in your backyard, the healthier your cities and homes are. They do not destroy the environment they live in. In fact, most make it a better place. If only we could say the same for ourselves.

Twinkle, twinkle little star,
There's a spider in the jar,
A gecko is munching on a fly,
All the black ants ate my pie.

ACKNOWLEDGEMENTS

Thank you . . .

Habiba, Razia and Rehana, my aunts—the rebels of the '50s and '60s who flew dragons much before I did!

Rafiq Tehsin, my lionhearted uncle with the longest moustaches!

My aunts Sakina and Shahre Banu, who have backyards that house all the wild possible (including cobras, believe me)

My fellow villagers at Creative Energy Unlimited (CEU) for reading each chapter with limitless energy

Buddy Boys, the terrific twins and the first critics of this book

Sohini and Purnima, my thorough, unflinching editors (eh . . . too many adjectives?)

And Saadat, my fellow pirate and explorer with whom, as a child, I explored all the wild in the backyard.

Cheers!

Arefa

http://arefatehsin.com/

BOOKS TO READ

Here are some books you can read if you wish to find out more about the wild in your backyard:

1. *Abbeville Press Encyclopedia of Natural Science* by Adriano Zanetti (Arnolo Mondadori Editore S.p.A., 1978)
2. *Handbook of the Birds of India and Pakistan Together with Those of Bangladesh, Nepal, Bhutan and Sri Lanka* by Salim Ali and S. Dillon Ripley (CBT and Oxford University Press, 1983)
3. *Mammalia of India: A New and Abridged Edition, Thoroughly Revised and with an Appendix on the Reptilia* by Frank Finn (Thacker Spink & Co., 1929)
4. *The Book of Indian Animals* by S.H. Prater (Bombay Natural History Society and Oxford University Press, 1990)
5. *The Book of Indian Birds* by Salim Ali (Bombay Natural History Society and Oxford University Press, 1977)
6. *The Encyclopedia of Vanished Species* by David Day (Mclaren Publishing [Hong Kong] Limited, 1989)
7. *The Illustrated Encyclopedia of Butterflies and Moths* by V.J. Stanek (Octopus Books Limited, 1977)

. . . and the Internet, of course.